Wallace Stevens and Company
The *Harmonium* Years
1913-1923

Studies in Modern Literature, No. 3

A. Walton Litz, General Series Editor

Consulting Editor for Titles on Wallace Stevens
Professor of English
Princeton University

Other Titles in This Series

No. 1   *Faulkner's Uses of the Classics*   Joan M. Serafin

No. 2   *A Touch of Rhetoric: Ezra Pound's
Malatesta Cantos*   Peter D'Epiro

No. 4   *The Latin Masks of Ezra Pound*   Ron Thomas

No. 5   *Studies in Joyce*   Nathan Halper

No. 6   *The Last Courtly Lover: Yeats and
the Idea of Woman*   Gloria C. Kline

No. 7   *William Carlos Williams: A Poet in
the American Theatre*   David A. Fedo

No. 8   *The Presence of the Past: T.S. Eliot's
Victorian Inheritance*   David Ned Tobin

No. 9   *A Thought to be Rehearsed: Aphorism in
Wallace Stevens's Poetry*   Beverly Coyle

No. 10   *Inverted Volumes Improperly Arranged:
James Joyce and His Trieste Library*   Michael Patrick Gillespie

Wallace Stevens and Company
The *Harmonium* Years
1913-1923

by
Glen G. MacLeod

UMI RESEARCH PRESS
Ann Arbor, Michigan

Quotations from the following works by Wallace Stevens are reprinted by permission of Alfred A. Knopf, Inc.: *The Collected Poems of Wallace Stevens, Letters of Wallace Stevens, The Necessary Angel, Opus Posthumous,* and *The Palm at the End of the Mind.*

The following works by William Carlos Williams are reprinted by permission of New Directions Publishing Corp.: "El Hombre," "Summer Song," "The Eyeglasses," "The Red Wheelbarrow," and "The Rose," from *Collected Earlier Poems of William Carlos Williams,* copyright © 1938 by William Carlos Williams; prose excerpts from *I Wanted to Write a Poem,* copyright © 1958 by William Carlos Williams; quotations from previously unpublished letters, copyright © 1983 by William Eric Williams and Paul H. Williams.

Quotations from *Amy Lowell: A Chronicle* by S. Foster Damon, copyright 1935 and renewed © 1963 by S. Foster Damon. Reprinted by permission of Houghton Mifflin Company.

For permission to quote from unpublished material by Wallace Stevens I am grateful to Holly Stevens.

For permission to quote previously unpublished material I am grateful to: Donald Gallup, literary trustee for Carl Van Vechten; the Witter Bynner Foundation for Poetry, Inc., literary executors for Witter Bynner; Barbara Ivins, literary executor for William M. Ivins, Jr.; and Mrs. Stanhope B. Vicke, literary executor for Arthur Davison Ficke.

For permission to quote from manuscripts in their collections, I wish to thank the following libraries and archives: The Beinecke Library, Yale University; The Houghton Library, Harvard University; The Huntington Library, San Marino, California; the Walter Conrad Arensberg Archives of the Philadelphia Museum of Art; and the Brown University Library.

Produced and distributed by
UMI Research Press
an imprint of
University Microfilms International
Ann Arbor, Michigan 48106

Library of Congress Cataloging in Publication Data

MacLeod, Glen G.
    Wallace Stevens and company.

        (Studies in modern literature ; no. 3)
        Revision of the author's thesis—Princeton University,
    1981.
        Bibliography: p.
        Includes index.
        1. Stevens, Wallace, 1879-1955—Friends and associates.
    2. Stevens, Wallace, 1879-1955. Harmonium. 3. Arts—
    York (N.Y.)—History—20th century. 4. New York (N.Y.)—
    Intellectual life.   I. Title. II. Series.
    PS3537.T4753Z677 1983   811'.52   83-3624
    ISBN 0-8357-1405-5

... There is about every poet a vast world of other people from which he derives himself and through himself his poetry.... His poetry is theirs and theirs is his, because of the interaction between the poet and his time....

Wallace Stevens

Contents

Acknowledgments   *ix*

Introduction   *xi*

Abbreviations   *xiii*

Part I: Stevens Among the Avant-Garde, 1913-1923

1   The "Patagonians" (1913-1915)   *3*

2   The "Art Crowd" (1914-1923)   *19*

Part II: Some Figures Behind Harmonium

3   Walter Conrad Arensberg   *45*

4   Eugène Emmanuel Lemercier   *55*

5   Donald Evans   *65*

6   William Carlos Williams   *77*

Conclusion   *93*

Notes   *95*

Bibliography   *109*

Index   *117*

Acknowledgments

During the course of my research and writing, I have been helped by many people. My greatest thanks go to A. Walton Litz, who first suggested the need for such a study, and whose own scholarship and exemplary direction have enabled me to undertake it. Thanks also go to Clarence Brown, in whose graduate seminar on Wallace Stevens I began the research that grew into this work. Like all Stevens scholars, I also owe a general debt of gratitude to Holly Stevens for her meticulous editing of the *Letters of Wallace Stevens* and *The Palm at the End of the Mind,* and for her thoughtful examination of her father's early life in *Souvenirs and Prophecies.* More particularly, I want to thank her for her kindness and encouragement while I have been working on this project.

I acknowledge gratefully the help of several other Stevens scholars: Milton Bates, Peter Brazeau, Robert Buttel, and Samuel French Morse read portions of this work-in-progress and gave me the benefit of their informed commentary. Joseph Riddel and Roy Harvey Pearce kindly replied to written queries.

In my research into the New York art world of the 1910s, Francis Naumann has been a model of scholarly cooperation. I also owe thanks to Richard Cary and Wallace I. Anderson for answering queries about Edwin Arlington Robinson; to John Sturdevant for answering queries about Donald Evans; to Chris MacGowan for helping with questions about William Carlos Williams; and to Bruce Gardiner for contributing some very useful observations about the British 1890s. One of my happiest debts is to Marion Meilaender whose friendship, encouragement, and practical advice have sustained me in instances too many to recall. And special thanks go to Louise Smith for her care in typing the manuscript.

The following people graciously consented to be interviewed about their connection with Stevens and/or his friends: the late Doris Fleischman Bernays; Edward L. Bernays; Irving Kolodin; Rebecca Reyher; Virgil Thomson; Louise Varèse; and Beatrice Wood.

I would like, finally, to thank the staffs of the following institutions for their help and cooperation during the course of my research: The Huntington Library, San Marino, California; the Beinecke Library, Yale University; the Princeton University Library; the Houghton Library, Harvard University; the John Hay Library, Brown University; the Trinity College Library; the Francis Bacon Library, Claremont, California; the Joseph Regenstein Library, University of Chicago; the McKeldin Library, University of Maryland; the Rare Book Room of the New York Public Library; the Harvard University Archives; the Haverford College Archives; and the Louise and Walter Arensberg Collection of the Philadelphia Museum of Art.

Introduction

The myth of Wallace Stevens as a shy and solitary figure composing poems in willful seclusion has, like most legends, some basis in fact. Stevens's shyness of publicity is well documented; and the rarity of personally revealing passages in his letters or journals confirms his fondness for privacy. But this legend has had an unfortunate influence on criticism of Stevens's poetry. Combined with Stevens's own repeated denials of any literary influences, and with the New Critical (and now Structuralist) emphasis on the isolated text, it has encouraged the reading of Stevens's poetry as hermetic, self-referential, and all but unrelated to his daily life, his acquaintances, or the artistic trends around him.

This method is useful insofar as it clarifies the distinctiveness of Stevens's poetic achievement. But it necessarily distorts our perception of Stevens, because it ignores the very context against which his distinction must be measured. And the resulting distortion is most serious in the case of Stevens's early work.

During the years 1913-23, while Stevens was writing the poems of *Harmonium*, he was more closely involved with other writers and artists than ever before or since. This was his most "experimental" phase; and his aesthetic point of reference was New York City, remaining so even after he moved to Hartford in 1916. Here, against the background of World War I and the early rise of modernism in the arts, Stevens conducted a deliberate search for his own poetic voice. As the poems of *Harmonium* were to become (in A. Walton Litz's phrase) "raw material" for Stevens's later refinement of style and theme, so his experience in New York during these years exemplifies the poetic concerns which shaped his entire career.

Stevens's own record of these years is scant. But we can broaden our understanding of his development by studying the larger movements within the New York art world of which he was part. And we can deepen that understanding by examining more closely his relationships with particular writers and artists. The following study is organized according to these two approaches.

Part I shows Stevens in the context of the literary/artistic groups he associated with during the *Harmonium* years. His first serious poetic efforts since college coincided with the general upsurge of avant-garde activity in New York following the Armory Show of 1913. He became associated, in this earliest period, with a group I shall call the "Patagonians": Donald Evans, Allen and Louise Norton, and Carl Van Vechten. This group's combination of Nineties elements with the literary innovations of Gertrude Stein provides an instructive parallel to Stevens's own poetic experiments of the time. But sometime in 1914-15, Stevens's attention was diverted to what became, for him, the center of avant-garde activity in New York City: the literary/artistic "salon" of his Harvard friend, Walter Conrad Arensberg. Here the lingering Nineties sensibility of the "Patagonians" mingled with the proto-Dada tendencies of the French expatriates (driven to New York by the war), producing the phenomenon known as New York Dada. The interests and activities of this group—and especially of its "guiding spirit," Marcel Duchamp—coincide strikingly with Stevens's own developing poetic interests. And the post-War disintegration of this "Art Crowd" provides a suggestive metaphor for the ending of Stevens's *Harmonium* period.

Part II, "Some Figures Behind *Harmonium*," focuses on Stevens's relations with individual writers. During the 1910s he entered into a series of virtual "collaborations" with other writers, and these provide the most dramatic instances of his openness to influence during this period. Walter Arensberg was not only a host and patron of the arts; he was also a good poet. His poetic interest in the relation between imagination and reality, and his love of Dante, both suggest an affinity with Wallace Stevens, which is confirmed by their actual collaboration on the poem, "Sonatina to Hans Christian." Eugène Emmanuel Lemercier was a French soldier/artist whose posthumous book *Lettres d'un Soldat* was the basis for Stevens's series of poems bearing the same title. Stevens's imaginative identification with Lemercier in this series adumbrates his later concern with the relation between soldier and poet, the clearest statement of which is the epilogue of "Notes toward a Supreme Fiction." Donald Evans is a forgotten poet with whom Stevens once planned to collaborate on a book of one-line poems; his spirit pervades "Le Monocle de Mon Oncle." And the last of these "collaborators" is William Carlos Williams, with whom Stevens exchanged advice, criticism, and praise throughout their separate careers.

These chapters represent only certain aspects of Wallace Stevens. Consider them, if you like, a series of snapshots of the developing poet at work. They do not attempt a single, definitive portrait. But together they may help to dispel the myth of Stevens as a poet in isolation. And they may suggest in Stevens's relation to his intellectual and aesthetic milieu a richness which deserves further study.

Abbreviations

The following abbreviations are used in the text and notes to denote Stevens's works.

CP   *The Collected Poems of Wallace Stevens.* New York: Knopf, 1954
L   *Letters of Wallace Stevens,* selected and edited by Holly Stevens. New York: Knopf, 1966
NA   *The Necessary Angel: Essays on Reality and the Imagination.* New York: Knopf, 1951
OP   *Opus Posthumous,* ed. Samuel French Morse. New York: Knopf, 1957
Palm   *The Palm at the End of the Mind: Selected Poems and a Play by Wallace Stevens,* ed. Holly Stevens. New York: Knopf, 1971; Vintage, 1972
SP   *Souvenirs and Prophecies: The Young Wallace Stevens.* New York: Knopf, 1977

The following abbreviations are used in the case of unpublished letters:
ALS   Autograph letter, signed
TLS   Typed letter, signed

Part I

Stevens Among the Avant-Garde
1913-1923

1

The "Patagonians" (1913-1915)

On August 7, 1913, Wallace Stevens wrote to his wife, who was spending the summer at Pocono Manor, Pennsylvania:

> I have ... been trying to get together a little collection of verses again; and although they are simple to read, when they're done, it's a deuce of a job (for me) to do them. Keep all this a great secret. There is something absurd about all this writing of verses; but the truth is, it elates and satisfies me to do it.... (*L*, 180)

Except for two negligible collections of lyrics written for his wife's birthday in 1908 and 1909, Stevens had not written poetry, so far as we know, since he left college in 1900. We should like to be able to say what factors contributed to this reawakening of poetic energy. But the record is virtually blank. We should also like to be sure whether, as seems likely, the verses he was "getting together" in the summer of 1913 were the "experimental" poems—like "Dolls," "Infernale," and "I have lived so long with the rhetoricians,"—which survive only in manuscript.[1] And perhaps more than anything in this earliest period of Stevens's mature poetic career, we should like to be able to explain the seemingly miraculous speed with which his talent developed from the slight or halting poems of 1913-14 to the masterful stanzas of "Sunday Morning" in 1915.

We shall never be able to answer these questions with certainty, unless unforeseen new evidence appears. What we can hope to do, however, is to fill in the background in greater detail than has yet been done—to clarify the context in which answers must be sought. In the present instance, that context is the group of writers Stevens was closest to in New York in 1913-15. If we gather together what we know of the lives of Stevens's literary friends during this period, we can achieve a "group portrait" whose general profile will provide at least a suggestive parallel to Stevens's own early development.

Doing so, we discover at once that in the summer of 1913, when Stevens was "trying to get together a little collection of verses," a group of New York writers with whom he would soon become involved were engaged in the same enterprise. Donald Evans, Allen and Louise Norton were spending the summer together at Congamond Lake in Massachusetts, relaxing, fishing—and writing.[2] The fourth member of this group, Carl Van Vechten, was spending the summer in Europe, but they sent him regular bulletins of their progress. On August 14, 1913—one week after Wallace Stevens wrote the above letter to his wife—Donald Evans wrote to Van Vechten:

> I have made Allen Norton work hard. He'll soon have a volume of poems ready and Louise I've teased until she too has just finished a short, choking one-act play, *Little Wax Candle,* which I am certain I can sell to the Princess Theatre. And I've been working beautifully, adorably, myself—a new volume ready for September 1 (for the publisher).[3]

These four people thought of themselves as a group. The three books they wrote that summer are full of private references, and are interconnected by allusions and dedications. Allen Norton's *Saloon Sonnets: With Sunday Flutings* is dedicated to Donald Evans and Louise Norton; it includes poems written to and about both of them; and its opening poem,"Chee Toy," deals with a character from Louise's play. His comic reference to "Congamuck Ponds" (i.e. Congamond Lake, p.22) would have been unintelligible outside their small circle. Donald Evans's *Sonnets from the Patagonian* includes sonnet-portraits of Van Vechten and the Nortons, and dedicates portraits of others to them. Louise Norton's play, *Little Wax Candle,* has three main characters: a married couple and their mutual friend, "Peter Peterson."[4] It reflects, in dramatic terms, the sophisticated attitudes and epigrammatic humor of Evans's and Allen Norton's sonnets, suggesting that these aspects of their literary pose may actually have colored their daily lives. I shall call this group the "Patagonians," after Donald Evans's conception of them. In using this term I shall mean quite specifically Evans, Van Vechten, and the Nortons during the years 1913-15, when Stevens would have known them as a definable group, and before his attention shifted (in 1915) to the newly-formed Arensberg salon (the subject of another chapter).

Stevens did not actually meet the Patagonians until late 1914, though by that time he knew their work well. They were published by Evans's short-lived Claire Marie Press in 1914 (the three books mentioned above comprised half its total list), and they were all involved with the magazine *Trend* in which Stevens's first published poems since college appeared during the same year. He did not know them in the summer of 1913.[5] But the course of events which led these people to spend that summer in literary pursuits may throw some light on Stevens's reasons for doing the same thing.

The story begins at Times Square, in the offices of the *New York Times.* There, in February 1913, Donald Evans, Allen Norton, and Carl Van Vechten were fellow-workers; and all three were dissatisfied, having literary ambitions beyond their present employment. By 1915 their lives would be greatly changed. By that year Donald Evans would have founded his own publishing house and moved to Philadelphia; Allen Norton would be editing his own magazine, *Rogue*; and Carl Van Vechten would have begun his new career as an author, publishing the first of a series of books which would appear on the average of one a year for the next seventeen years. But in February of 1913 all three men were simply frustrated with their present careers.

Donald Evans, a native of Philadelphia, had come to the *Times* in 1912, after seven years with the *Philadelphia Inquirer*. He was nearly thirty years old, and was married. To the casual eye he appeared the embodiment of the average newspaperman: "When I first met him," recalled Van Vechten, "Donald was a copyreader on the *New York Times,* conventionally dressed and with conventional manners."[6] In fact, however, he was only enduring newspaper work as a necessary stage in the literary career he had been planning for himself since he dropped out of Haverford College in 1903.[7] His first volume of poems, *Discords* (Philadelphia: N.L. Brown), had finally been published in 1912, and he had immediately moved to New York to begin a new literary life as a published poet. But now, nearly a year later, he was stalled. He found himself mired in journalistic routine, and had not written a poem since leaving Philadelphia. Events would soon conspire to change this situation.

In the same building, and in much the same mood, was Allen Norton. He was younger than Evans, about twenty-three, but like him had dropped out of college (Harvard, 1910) to go into journalism; and he, too, had greater literary ambitions.[8] His wife, née Louise McCutcheon, had dropped out of Smith College to marry Allen in 1911. The couple both came from well-to-do families—they were listed in the New York Social Register for 1913—but both were bored with respectability. Allen wanted to be a writer of books, and Louise wanted the excitement of a literary life, to be among the interesting and "peculiar" people she had never known in her conventional family.[9] Because they had some independent income, Allen had been able to take a leave of absence from the *Times* in the fall of 1912, and the couple had spent several months in Ormonde, Florida, where Allen devoted his time to writing stories. They would do the same thing in the spring of 1913. But the stories were not getting published, and there was not much literary life to be had in Ormonde, Florida. They, too, were ripe for a change.

The senior member of this inchoate alliance was Carl Van Vechten. Born in the Midwest, he had been a journalist in Chicago before coming to New York in 1906 as an Assistant Music Critic for the *Times*. Seven years later, at the age of thirty-three, he still held that position, but his interests were not much engaged by his professional duties. He was more interested in meeting "amusing" people, and in writing about them. Mabel Dodge recorded her impressions of Van Vechten at this time:

He amused me because he had such a sense of humor and was so full of life.... With him 'amusing' things were essential things; whimsicality was the note they must sound to have significance. Life was perceived to be a fastidious circus, and strange conjunctions were more prized than the ordinary relationships rooted in eternity.[10]

Van Vechten most enjoyed socializing, and he excelled as an entertaining social commentator, as his later novels attest. When the "Patagonians" came into being, he naturally took the role of "biographer of the movement."[11]

In February, 1913, two things happened to bring together the lives of Donald Evans, the Nortons, and Carl Van Vechten. The most spectacular of these was the Armory Show, which opened at the Sixty-Ninth Regiment Armory in New York on February 17, 1913. We are fortunate enough to have Van Vechten's own recollection of the event:

> This show has now become almost a legend but it was the reality of that winter. It was the first, and possibly the last, exhibition of paintings held in New York which everybody attended. Everybody went and everybody talked about it. Street-car conductors asked your opinion of the Nude Descending the Staircase, as they asked you for your nickel . . . the show was a bang-up, whale of a success. . . . It was cartooned, it was caricatured . . . John Wanamaker advertised cubist gowns and ladies began to wear green, blue, and violet wigs, and to paint their faces emerald and purple. The effects of this aesthetic saturnalia are manifest even today.[12]

This passage occurs in Van Vechten's novel, *Peter Whiffle* (1922), so the gowns, wigs, and makeup may be fictional. But in any case it shows as keen an interest in the "strange" as the narrator of Stevens's "Disillusionment of Ten O'Clock," who dreams of nightgowns colored "green,/ Or purple with green rings,/ Or green with yellow rings,/ Or yellow with blue rings." Van Vechten recalls the Armory Show as a victory for the imagination, pointing the way to all that is strange and new and modern. We may consider this reaction typical of all the "Patagonians."

At the same time, however, Van Vechten was clearly aware—as a journalist himself—of how great a part publicity played in the success of the show. The new art often seemed deliberately to thumb its nose at public taste, and to eschew popularity; yet it became popular with the public for that very reason. The outrage it inspired made good "copy." It sold newspapers. And that publicity helped, inadvertently, to create an audience for modern art. The many came to jeer, but they paid their admission fees; and the few serious buyers came, too. This point was not lost on the "Patagonians," who as newsmen were in a good position to promote their own work. Evans, for instance, suggested the following plan to Van Vechten in a letter of January 27, 1914:

> Merritt, editor of the magazine (Sunday) of the American would run a page story on the Patagonian Sonnets, if a story with photographs could be worked up that all the people portrayed are getting ready to sue me for libel and to have the book suppressed. The suit needn't actually have to be filed. Do you suppose it could be done? . . . [13]

This particular plan never materialized, but it shows that these would-be-writers were wondering how the lessons of the Armory Show could be applied in the realm of literature.

As if anticipating exactly this question, another event occurred in February, 1913, which was much quieter but no less important to the "Patagonians." A few days before the Armory Show, Carl Van Vechten first read Gertrude Stein's "Portrait of Mabel Dodge at the Villa Curonia," and he immediately began showing it to his friends.[14] The "Portrait" was generally received as a literary equivalent of the new painting, and this impression was strengthened when it was reprinted in a special issue of *Camera Work* (June 1913) devoted to the Armory Show. It must have seemed proof that the refreshing strangeness of modern art was also possible in literature.[15]

It is difficult to overestimate the impact of this discovery on the "Patagonians." Donald Evans was inspired to write his first poem in nearly a year, the first of a series of sonnet-"portraits" in the oblique Stein manner which are the most accomplished work of his career; and he arranged to have Stein's *Tender Buttons* published by his own Claire Marie Press the next year. Allen Norton began writing sonnet-portraits, too; and his magazine, *Rogue,* would publish work by Gertrude Stein. Carl Van Vechten quit his job at the *Times* in May of 1913, and sailed to Europe to stay at the Villa Curonia for the summer and to meet Gertrude Stein. They became friends immediately, and remained so over the years; she eventually named him her literary executor.

A brief excerpt from the beginning of the "Portrait of Mabel Dodge at the Villa Curonia" will illustrate Stein's method:

> So much breathing has not the same place when there is that much beginning. So much breathing has the same place and there must not be so much suggestion. There can be there the habit that there is if there is no need of resting. The absence is not alternative.
>
> Any time is the half of all the noise and there is not that disappointment. There is no distraction. An argument is clear.[16]

One's first impression is of a very self-conscious style. The simple words, the plainness of the constructions, and the repetition point forward—as is well known—to the spare prose of Ernest Hemingway. But the disjunction between Stein's earnest rhetorical control and the seeming nonsense it conveys has a primarily comic effect, in this instance, which also looks forward to the very opposite tendency in American writing—the robust luxuriance of *Harmonium.* Mabel Dodge defends Stein's "portraits" and the painting of the Cubists with the same argument: "That there has been an *approach* is what counts. It is only in a state of indifference that there is no approach at all, and indifference reeks of death."[17] This is the underlying rationale of all modernist experimentation, including Stevens's own development during the 1910s.

The effect of Stein's style on the "Patagonians" may be measured by the case of Donald Evans. The poems of his first book had been conventional exercises in the Nineties manner. Here is one:

JADIS ET NAGUERE

When disillusionment was fiercely new
I wildly prayed at night upon my knees
That I might cease to care he was untrue.

My heart was bursting with love's agonies;
I longed for a numbed sense to ease my pain,
And a dull sleep to still my soul's lorn cries.

I said unto my soul: —This grief must wane,
And bring dumb hours when thou wilt feel naught,
Except that the days pass in endless train.

I did not know at what a price I sought
To buy escape. But now I know full well
How bitter is the peace that I have bought.

With husband here I am content to dwell,
And he has not changed; still untrue he is,
And yet no hot wrath makes my heart rebel.

My depth of degradation is in this, —
That I feel lonely when he is away,
And when he returns thrill under his kiss!

The French title from Verlaine, the emphasis on the "degradation" of sexual passion, the bitter world-weariness, the archaic diction ("thou wilt"), hackneyed phrasing ("lorn cries"), and inversions ("untrue he is")—all derive from the Nineties, though this poem was not published until 1912. But observe the change from this to Evans's first "Patagonian" sonnet, written in the winter of 1913 while, according to Carl Van Vechten, "the name of Gertrude Stein was ringing loudly in his ears".[18]

LOVE IN PATAGONIA

Forgetting her mauve vows the Fania fled,
Taking away her moonlight scarves with her—
There was no joy left in the calendar,
And life was just an orchid that was dead.
Even our pious peacocks went unfed—
I had deserved no treachery like this,
For I had bitten sharp kiss after kiss
Devoutly, till her sleek young body bled.

Then Carlo came; he shone like a new sin—
Straightway I knew pearl-powder still was sweet,
And that my bleeding heart would not be scarred.
I sought a shop where shoes were sold within,
And for two hundred francs made brave my feet,
And then I danced along the boulevard!

The "Frenchness" is still here ("francs," boulevard"), the emphasis on sexual passion, and the mannered show of grief. But the style has been radically transformed. The change is evident even in the title, which is as oblique as Stein's "Portrait of Mabel Dodge at the Villa Curonia," that mentions neither Mabel Dodge nor the Villa Curonia. There are no more inversions, but a simplified sentence structure and a correspondingly greater suppleness of rhythm. The new Evans avoids hackneyed phrasing, searching instead for strange conjunctions of words ("mauve vows," "moonlight scarves," "pious peacocks"). And instead of archaic diction, which invoked a familiar "literary" past, the diction here is idiosyncratic ("bitten... devoutly," "shone like a... sin"), creating the sense of an imaginative realm—a "Patagonia"—where such odd combinations might really exist.

This sonnet contains the germ of Evans's sequence, the *Sonnets from the Patagonian*. It is the only poem in that book not titled "Portrait of...," perhaps because its subjects are named in the poem itself: "the Fania" is Fania Marinoff, who married "Carlo" Van Vechten in 1914. One hesitates to say in what sense Evans intended to convey the actual personalities of this couple, but his friends sometimes did assume that his sonnets were meant to be recognizable portraits. About one of his "Portraits of Louise Norton," Arthur Davison Ficke wrote: "Since I have come to know Louise better, I admire even more than before the extraordinary loveliness of 'The Jade Vase.'"[19] But for the average reader the personality which comes across most strongly in all of the Patagonian sonnets is that of the narrator. Van Vechten once remarked that Evans's letters "are really WRITTEN to himself," and in reading his sonnets we are likely to conclude similarly that most of them are autobiographical.[20] In the same way, of course, it might be said that Stein's "Portraits" of others are really self-portraits, as the famous *Autobiography of Alice B. Toklas* is really the autobiography of Gertrude Stein. Both Stein and Evans narrate their "portraits" in an idiosyncratic style which conveys a quirky, comic personality. The same impulse is evident in the most characteristic poems of Wallace Stevens's *Harmonium*—e.g., "Bantams in Pine Woods," "Le Monocle de Mon Oncle," and "The Comedian as the Letter C"—where the humorously skewed language is the fitting expression of an odd but fully realized persona.

Stevens was surely aware in 1913 of the innovations of the Armory Show and of Stein's prose; and he almost certainly knew of the "Patagonians" through his good friend from Harvard, Pitts Sanborn, who as fellow music critic, knew Carl Van Vechten well. (In fact, when Van Vechten sailed to Europe to meet Gertrude Stein in May, 1913, Sanborn was one of his shipmates.)[21] But whether these particular events, or some more general modernist *Zeitgeist,* or simply private inclinations most influenced Stevens's emerging style, we cannot say. What is certain is that Stevens shared with the Patagonians a predisposition for the Nineties mode. Donald Evans described the "new spirit" of the 1910s as the "true child of the brave and battlesome 'Yellow 90s' of England," and the rest of his group clearly agreed with him.[22] Their "modernization" superimposed an idiosyncratic, modernist style on elements familiar from the Nineties. This pattern applies as well to many of Steven's *Harmonium* poems.

The Patagonians' respect for the Nineties was, at the time, a minority opinion. The prevailing attitude among serious readers of poetry is exemplified by *Poetry*'s review of *Sonnets from the Patagonian* and *Saloon Sonnets* in October, 1914:

> There are signs of a late grafting of the spirit of the eighteen-nineties upon certain young poets of the United States. Of course we have had earlier and more authentic indications of that spirit in poets whose work is based upon artistic methods of the nineties, but the grafting of which I speak represents rather a tendency to imitate only that phrase of the cult whose literary trademark is the sophistication of wickedness. . . .

> Not a little of this foolish and rather wasteful child's play, in combination with certain post-impressionist leanings, is found in the two volumes of poems by Mr. Donald Evans and Mr. Allen Norton.[23]

Later in the review, the reviewer (Alice Corbin Henderson) praises Evans's gift for phrasing and his "natural vigor," but most of her energy goes into criticizing the Patagonians' desire to *épater le bourgeois.* This tendency was what the Nineties signified to most people in the 1910s, and both advanced and conservative critics agreed in disliking it. Amy Lowell wrote of Evans's *Sonnets* when they were reissued in 1918:

> . . . I lived during the 1890's. My twenty years saw the annual reappearance of "The Yellow Book," and these "mauve joys" and "purple sins" were the very "latest thing" during my adolescent period so that I must be pardoned for finding their manner somewhat dusty and, indeed, a good deal like a cotillion favor resurrected from a bureau drawer. . . .[24]

If such champions of modern verse professed to be bored by these "purple sins," the newspaper critics still tended to be outraged by them. The New York *Morning Telegraph* reviewed Louise Norton's *Little Wax Candle,* but refused to summarize its plot, considering it indecent.[25] And the conservative reaction to Evan's *Sonnets* is summarized in a survey of contemporary poetry published in 1918:

> ... To the orthodox he was a mad man, "a futurist charlatan," "an insincere poseur," "a monster of salacity," ... Such lines as
>
>> For I had bitten sharp kiss after kiss
>> Devoutly, till her sleek young body bled.
>> ......
>> Then Carlo came; he shone like a new sin.
>
> certainly were destined to stir up a Puritanical ripple among those accustomed to traditional ways. As for "In The Vices" [another of the *Sonnets*], these lines brought upon his head the accusation of sheer vulgarity.[26]

All these criticisms are directed at the Nineties' desire to *épater,* which the Patagonians insisted was still valid. They were right, in theory, if we think of the successful career of Dada as an extension of this desire; but in practice, their manner was generally unoriginal and therefore ineffective. We do not usually think of Wallace Stevens in connection with this aspect of the Nineties, but for a brief period during 1914, while he was watching the progress of the Patagonians, Stevens, too, experimented in this mode. He toyed with the "shocking" topics of sacrilege and sexuality in the manuscript poem, "Dolls" (which we shall consider in more detail below), and in "Cy Est Pourtraicte . . . ," which comically confuses religious and sexual devotion. In this latter poem, St. Ursula addresses God as "My dear," and He responds with "a subtle quiver,/ That was not heavenly love,/ Or pity." This was one of the poems Stevens read aloud late in 1914, at a party at the Walter Arensbergs', where the other guests were Carl Van Vechten, Fania Marinoff, and the Nortons.[27] Allen Norton remembered the recitation, and several months later got Stevens's permission to publish "Cy Est Pourtraicte..." in the first issue of his magazine, *Rogue* (March 15, 1915).[28]

Stevens quickly abandoned this *fin de siècle* naughtiness, but his affection for the Nineties remained; it was not limited to such superficial mannerisms. His college poems had been *written* in the 1890s, and naturally exhibited many traits common to that period.[29] And the first published poems of his mature career, in 1914, still exhibit the delicate, twilit mood one associates with the Nineties. A. Walton Litz points out the "Yeatsian" theme of the *Trend* poem, "Home Again":

> It was evidently Stevens's intention in "Home Again" to express a theme very like that of Yeats'"Lake Isle of Innisfree"; in a letter to his fiancée written early in 1909 he spoke of "the cottage" as "the youthful ideal of all Men," and clinched his point by quoting from Yeats' poem:

'Where morn is all aglimmer
And noon a purple glow
And evening, full of the linnet's wings.'[30]

Like Yeats, Stevens would soon make a deliberate effort to break out of his
early manner. But unlike many other modernist writers (Ezra Pound and
William Carlos Williams immediately come to mind), he did not entirely
disavow the Nineties in his maturity. He agreed with the Patagonians in valuing
fine phrasing and epigram for their own sakes; had a taste for the exotic—
strange places, words, things; and appreciated the poetic uses of artificiality
and theatricality. All these stylistic elements of the Nineties characterize
Harmonium, and survive to some degree in his later work.

The example of Yeats is crucial in this regard. He was something of an
anomaly among the younger poets of the revolutionary 1910s, who tended to
define themselves against the otherworldliness of the 1890s. Yeats had been a
leading exponent of the "Celtic twilight" in the Nineties, and he was now, in
1914, the reigning poet in the English language. His attitude toward the
Nineties is epitomized by his poem, "The Grey Rock," which appeared in
Poetry in April, 1913. Here Yeats counterpoints the names of Nineties poets
with figures from Irish folklore, making legendary heroes of the men who had
(with Yeats) formed the Rhymers Club:

You had to face your ends when young—
'Twas wine or women, or some curse—
But never made a poorer song
That you might have a heavier purse,
Nor gave loud service to a cause
That you might have a troop of friends.
You kept the Muses' sterner laws,
And unrepenting faced your ends,
And earned the right—and yet
Dowson and Johnson most I praise—
To troop with those the world's forgot,
And copy their proud steady gaze.[31]

The Nineties represented to Yeats a spirit of fierce dedication to poetic ideals,
even to the point of self-destruction. His later essay about these same poets
would be titled, appropriately, "The Tragic Generation."[32] This view of the
Nineties would also inform Ezra Pound's "Hugh Selwyn Mauberley" (1920) in
which he contrasted the venal spirit of the modern age as he saw it—"an old
bitch gone in the teeth," "a botched civilization"—with the firm idealism of the
Nineties. As one spineless contemporary puts it in Pound's poem:

Don't kick against the pricks,
Accept opinion. The "Nineties" tried your game
And died, there's nothing in it.

Recent critics have tended to confirm the view of the Nineties, not as a period of decadence, but as a period of remarkable vitality, out of which emerged the major currents of modern poetry.[33] It was a view surely sympathetic to Wallace Stevens.

But in the early 1910s, the loudest voices of the modernist movement were directed squarely against the *fin de siècle*. The single most effective campaign for modernist reform took place under the banner of Imagism, a doctrine explicitly designed to combat the twilit atmosphere and vague phrasing which characterized Yeats's early verse. And the chief exponent of Imagism was Ezra Pound himself who served as the London correspondent of *Poetry*. It is one of the ironies of literary history that he was also, during the years 1913-15, Yeats's personal secretary, and was responsible for the regular appearance of Yeats's poems in *Poetry*.[34] The close relationship between Pound and Yeats during these years demonstrates an unusual willingness, on the part of both men, to overlook ephemeral "winds of doctrine" (a phrase popularized by Santayana's book of that title, published in 1913) in the dispassionate pursuit of genuine poetry. Reviewing Yeats's *Responsibilities* for *Poetry* in May, 1914, Pound wrote:

> ... whenever I mention Mr. Yeats I am apt to be assailed with questions: "Will Mr. Yeats do anything more?", "Is Yeats in the movement?", "How *can* the chap go on writing this sort of thing?"
>
> And to these inquiries I can only say that Mr. Yeats' vitality is quite unimpaired, and that I dare say he'll do a good deal; and that up to date no one has shown any disposition to supersede him as the best poet in England, or any likelihood of doing so for some time; ... and that there is no need for a poet to repair each morning of his life to the *Piazza dei Signori* to turn a new sort of somersault; and that Mr. Yeats is so assuredly an immortal that there is no need for him to recast his style to suit our winds of doctrine ...[35]

These may seem remarkable concessions from the champion of modernism whose motto was "make it new," and who was more apt to spend his time *fanning* "winds of doctrine" than ignoring them. This passage amounts to a defense of Yeats's formal conservatism against the more intolerant advocates of "free verse." And it anticipates Pound's own use of strict form in "Hugh Selwyn Mauberley," in reaction against the laxness he deplored in much of the new writing.

But Pound devotes most of his review of *Responsibilities* to discussing the "manifestly new note in [Yeats's] later work." He detects a new "hardness of outline" in his book, and explicitly contrasts it with the Nineties mode:

> ... I've not a word against the glamour as it appears in Yeats' early poems, but we have had so many other pseudo-glamours and glamourlets and mists and fogs since the nineties that one is about ready for hard light.[36]

This "hard light" was congenial to Imagism, but Yeats had come to it on his own. Since the publication of *The Wind Among the Reeds* (1899), Yeats had been moving away from the "glamour" of his early style. His experience writing for the theater led him to seek a more vigorous mode of expression in his non-dramatic verse, as his "Preface" to *Poems: 1899-1905* (1906) explains:

> ... to me drama—and I think it has been the same with other writers—has been the search for more of manful energy, more of cheerful acceptances of whatever arises out of the logic of events, and for clean outline, instead of those outlines of lyric poetry that are blurred with desire and vague regret.[37]

This new "manful energy" and "clean outline" is what Pound singles out for praise as a "quality of hard light" in one of Yeats's poems which appeared in the same issue of *Poetry,* "The Magi":

> Now as at all times I can see in the mind's eye,
> In their stiff, painted clothes, the pale unsatisfied ones
> Appear and disappear in the blue depth of the sky
> With all their ancient faces like rain-beaten stones,
> And all their helms of silver hovering side by side,
> And all their eyes still fixed, hoping to find once more,
> Being by Calvary's turbulence unsatisfied,
> The uncontrollable mystery on the bestial floor.

The "hardness" Pound points out here is especially effective because it emphasizes the theme of the poem. Yeats depicts the failure of our traditional mythologies (specifically Christianity) by focusing on the "unsatisfied" mythical figures whose promise has remained unfulfilled; now they have stiffened to caricatures of themselves, hovering half-glimpsed "in the blue depth of the sky."

Stevens hardly needed Pound to point out to him the remarkable achievement of this poem. The theme was as important to Stevens as to Yeats. And the younger poet, who had himself been practicing to achieve the virtues of Imagism, could not have failed to admire Yeats's confident treatment of so broad a theme in the form of a single, concrete image. The selection of poems from *Responsibilities* in *Poetry* of May, 1914, must have whetted Stevens's desire to see the complete book. Perhaps with this in mind he wrote to Yeats's Cuala Press that summer requesting their circulars.[38] Meanwhile, although the American edition of *Responsibilities* was not available until 1916, he did have access to a copy of the Cuala Press edition: the New York Public Library acquired a copy of *Responsibilities* in the summer of 1914, when Stevens—a regular patron of the Library—could easily have read it.[39] In this book "The Magi" is paired with a poem called "The Dolls," and Yeats appends a note explaining the relation between the two poems:

The fable for this poem came into my head while I was giving some lectures in Dublin. I had noticed once again how all thought among us is frozen into "something other than human life." After I had made the poem, I looked up one day into the blue of the sky, and suddenly imagined, as if lost in the blue of the sky, stiff figures in procession. I remembered that they were the habitual image suggested by blue sky, and looking for a second fable called them "The Magi," complementary forms to those enraged dolls.[40]

In "The Dolls," as Richard Ellman paraphrases the poem, "the doll-maker's house is thrown into an uproar by the complaints of the dolls at the introduction of a real baby into the house."[41] It is an image of "dead" convention obstructing any genuine new life. Yeats extended this idea, in "The Magi," to include the religious conventions of Christianity, which seemed to him to have become as lifeless as those dolls.

Dolls were a familiar image in the art of the time: Maeterlinck wrote plays for marionettes; and in New York, Alfred Kreymborg had a puppet-theater and wrote a play ("Lima Beans") which required the actors to move like puppets. Painters like Duchamp, Picabia, and Schamberg were experimenting with mechanomorphic images; John Covert, whom Stevens knew, actually did paintings of dolls titled "Dolls" (ca. 1915) and "Water Babies" (1919). For Yeats, the image of "dolls" was connected with the self-conscious artifice of the the 1890s. His poem, "Upon a Dying Lady" (1912-14), uses dolls specifically as emblems of the Nineties: Artists are depicted bringing dolls to the deathbed of Mabel Beardsley, sister of the artist, Aubrey Beardsley; and the actual dolls which inspired this poem were "dressed like people out of her brother's drawings," as Yeats informed Lady Gregory.[42] Wallace Stevens, too, associated "dolls" with the Nineties. And his manuscript poem, "Dolls," seems clearly to have been written with Yeats's "The Magi" and "The Dolls" (and their accompanying note) in mind:

> The thought of Eve, within me, is a doll
> That does what I desire, as, to perplex,
> With apple-buds, the husband in her sire.
>
> There's a pious caliph, now, who prays and sees
> A vermeil cheek. He is half-conscious of
> The quaint seduction of a scented veil.
>
> Playing with dolls? A solid game, greybeards.
> Think of cherubim and seraphim,
> And of Another, whom I must not name.[43]

Stevens has incorporated both the concept (from "The Dolls") of "dolls" as lifeless abstractions of real men (the "thought of Eve" rather than Eve herself), and the concept (from "The Magi") of "dolls" as religious icons that have lost their original power (e.g. "Cherubim and seraphim"). Stevens's theme is the same as that of "The Magi"—the failure of religious belief; and like Yeats he sees his mythological figures only "in the mind's eye" ("within me"). But Stevens's humorously ironic approach is quite different from that of Yeats. Stevens draws out the sexual innuendo in the word, "doll" (the slang term for any attractive woman),[44] and adopts a tone of coy suggestiveness that might have pleased Aubrey Beardsley. Ironically, the poem Pound singled out for its distance from the Nineties has become the occasion for a reversion to *fin de siècle* naughtiness. A more descriptive title for this poem might be, "Nuances of a Theme by Yeats in the Patagonian Manner."

Like several of Stevens's poems in 1914, "Dolls" has what Harriet Monroe called "a kind of modern-gargoyle grin" about it, but such grotesquerie alone is not enough to carry the poem.[45] The trouble with "Dolls" becomes clear if we ask, Who is "Another" in the final line? Is it the Virgin Mary, appropriate in this sacrilegious context as a "doll" to balance "Eve" in the first line? Or is it the Christ child, once the object of the Magi's fixed gaze, and an infant like the one which outraged Yeats's dolls? Or is it God himself whom, in the Old Testament tradition, "I must not name"? The problem is not very interesting, for the poem's statement would be much the same in any case. Stevens is indulging in coyness for its own sake, and is ambiguous to little purpose.

"Dolls" is an experimental poem. In it we can see elements of the Nineties and the more recent Patagonian modes; but it also looks forward, in both theme and style, to the great poems of Stevens's *Harmonium* period. This early use of the doll-image surely lies behind the eleventh stanza of "Le Monocle de Mon Oncle," which begins: "If sex were all, then every trembling hand/ Could make us squeak, like dolls, the wished-for words." As Robert Buttel notes, "Dolls" treats the same theme as "Monocle"—"the interdependence of the sexual and the spiritual"—and so may be viewed as a model for that later poem.[46] And "Monocle" itself may be seen as Stevens's triumphant coming-to-terms with the poetic impulses which drew him, in 1914, to experiment with *fin de siècle* "naughtiness."

In taking for its theme the failure of religious beliefs in the modern world, "Dolls" also anticipates "Sunday Morning." It may seem unlikely that the adolescent coyness of Stevens's "experimental" poem of 1914 should lead so quickly to the stately self-possession of his masterpiece of 1915. But Yeats's "The Magi" stands in the background of both poems (as it stands behind Yeats's own "The Second Coming"), and it is the intensely meditative power of that poem which informs "Sunday Morning." The third stanza of Stevens's poem even recurs to the imagery of "The Magi," where "the pale unsatisfied ones/ Appear and disappear in the blue depth of the sky": Here the mythical figure is Jove, who once had an "inhuman" birth "in the clouds," but has since then faded from sight, leaving the sky a "dividing and indifferent blue."

Perhaps it was necessary for Stevens to commit the excesses of "Dolls"— to give free rein to these Nineties mannerisms in order to see where they would lead him, and finally to discard them. In the same way, it may have been necessary for Stevens to encounter the "Patagonians," and to come to terms with their peculiar poetic tendencies in himself, before he could define his own personal style in poems as different as "Le Monocle de Mon Oncle" and "Sunday Morning."

By the time Wallace Stevens met the Patagonians, in December of 1914, they were already drifting apart. The Claire Marie Press, which published their books, had folded in September, and *Trend* would publish its last issue in February, 1915. Donald Evans—the "Prince" of this group, as Alfred Kreymborg called him[47]—soon went his own way: When the Nortons began their new magazine, *Rogue,* in March of 1915, he was not included; and by the end of 1915 he had moved back to Philadelphia. Wallace Stevens, in any case, was quickly tiring of the Patagonians' excesses, in both art and life. Writing to Elsie on August 3, 1915, he complained that Carl Van Vechten had "absolutely no sense that enough is enough" (*L,* 185). It is a mark of the real temperamental difference between these two men that Van Vechten would cheerfully have agreed with Stevens's assessment: he even had personal stationery printed up, with the motto, "A little too much is just enough for me."[48] In 1915 the brief alliance of the Patagonians ended, and they—along with Wallace Stevens—directed their attention, instead, towards the new literary/ artistic "salon" of Walter Conrad Arensberg.

2

The "Art Crowd" (1914-1923)

Early in 1922, Wallace Stevens donated his entire collection of art catalogues to the Wadsworth Atheneum in Hartford. These catalogues comprised, by Stevens's own account, a virtually complete record of every important art exhibit in New York during the preceding decade; and now he was getting rid of them. This gesture marks the formal end to an important aspect of Stevens's life during the years in which he wrote the poems of *Harmonium*—his involvement with the group he referred to as the "art crowd."[1] Though he retained his interest in art throughout his life, Stevens was never again so closely associated with a particular group of artists as he was for nearly ten years during the 1910s. The "art crowd," for Wallace Stevens, meant primarily the group of writers and artists who used to gather at the apartment of his old friend, Walter Conrad Arensberg, at 33 West 67th Street in New York. It was here that the Society of Independent Artists was created in 1917, and here the movement known as New York Dada had its headquarters. From just after the Armory Show to the time Arensberg abandoned New York for California in 1921, Stevens was a frequent guest at this salon. The character of the group, and the interests of its members, formed an important part of the intellectual and aesthetic background from which *Harmonium* developed.

The birth of the modern movement in American poetry is usually dated 1912, the year Harriet Monroe founded her Chicago-based magazine, *Poetry*. From the very beginning, this "new poetry" was recognized as an avant-garde movement related to similar movements in the other arts: "Our twentieth century poetry... reflects the exhilarating trend that is sweeping over Continental music, painting and poetry," announced the editor of *The Lyric Year* (1912).[2] This forward-looking anthology was published, appropriately, in New York City—"appropriately" because at the time New York was the only city in the United States in which the European avant-garde artists had been exhibited. Here, from as early as 1908, Alfred Stieglitz's Photo-Secession Gallery at 291 Fifth Avenue had been showing works by Matisse, Rodin, Picasso, and others.[3] And soon, in February of 1913, New York would host the Armory Show, the exhibit which introduced the American public to Post-

Impressionism and Cubism, and which would come to be known as "the most important single exhibition ever held in America."[4]

The upsurge of interest in avant-garde art in New York during the 1910s coincides with the appearance of Wallace Stevens's first mature poems. Much has been written about the relations between Stevens's poetry and painting, but the possible connections between the poetry of *Harmonium* and the group of artists whom Stevens knew during the time of its composition remains to be explored.[5]

Stevens's retiring manner and his disinclination to be included in any "group" are legendary, so that the very notion of his attending social gatherings with any regularity may seem out of character. But his connection with the Arensberg circle is a special case. It was natural for Stevens to visit the Arensbergs' "salon" in their apartment at 33 West 67th Street, because he and Walter Arensberg were close friends. Their friendship began in college, and flowered during the 1910s when both were living in New York. Stevens wrote of that time: "Walter and I were good friends over a long period of years and I saw a lot of him and his wife. I liked them both" (*L,* 850).[6] The closeness of their friendship, on Stevens's part at least, is shown by his unusually fine memory, in later years, of Arensberg's New York activities. Writing in 1954 to Fiske Kimball, who was compiling a biography of Arensberg for the Philadelphia Museum of Art, Stevens displayed a more informed knowledge of Arensberg and his circle than any of Kimball's other sources, excepting only Arensberg's brother, Charles.[7]

Walter Conrad Arensberg and Wallace Stevens were fellow Pennsylvanians, a fact which mattered to both men: Stevens felt throughout his life a deep attachment to the landscape around Reading; and Arensberg, born in Pittsburgh in 1878, donated to the Philadelphia Museum of Art his invaluable art collection, at least partly out of devotion to his home state.[8] They attended Harvard together, leaving in the same year, 1900. Their shared inclinations toward both art and literature are evidenced by the two courses they took together while at Harvard: *English 7* (1898-99), a full-year survey course in Eighteenth Century English Literature; and *Fine Arts 4* (1899-1900), a one-semester course in the art of the Middle Ages and Renaissance.[9] Both men worked on college literary magazines, as Stevens remembered years later: "When I first came to know [Walter] in Cambridge, he was active on the *Monthly,* and I was active on the *Advocate*" (*L,* 820). Stevens began working on the *Advocate* early in 1899.[10] If, as seems likely, Arensberg was editing the *Monthly* at the same time, it is possible he had something to do with the pseudonymous printing, in the July and December *Monthly,* of two sonnets by Wallace Stevens.[11]

Stevens speculated about the chief influences, at Harvard, on Arensberg's intellectual development: "Probably Charles Eliot Norton had considerable influence on him although he was probably also influenced by Santayana" (*L,* 820). As students, both men had known Santayana—Arensberg took his course in *Aesthetics* during his Senior year, and Stevens "came to know him a little" through informal conversations.[12] The "Old Philosopher" clearly meant a great deal to Stevens, so that his mention of Santayana in connection with Arensberg is the acknowledgment of a common bond. Arensberg's connection with Charles Eliot Norton may go even deeper, however. Norton founded the Department of Fine Arts at Harvard, though he retired from teaching in 1898 before either Stevens or Arensberg had studied in that department. But Norton's spirit lingered and extended well beyond the Art Department, so that the future art collector, Arensberg, must have felt and responded to Norton's exemplary dedication to art. Another of Norton's major interests was Italian literature, and he published a respected prose translation of the *Divine Comedy* in 1891-92.[13] Arensberg certainly shared his enthusiasm for Dante, and perhaps even surpassed it, for he undertook the task of translating the entire *Divine Comedy* into English terza-rima; and he spent years developing his own elaborately cryptographic and symbolic reading of Dante.[14] It can hardly have been pure chance that, upon Norton's death in 1908, Walter Arensberg and his recent bride moved into the famous scholar's former home, "Shady Hill," in Cambridge, where they lived until moving to New York in 1914.[15]

We know that Stevens and Arensberg had at least one good friend in common while at Harvard: Pitts Sanborn (Class of 1900), who was to remain close to both men until his death in 1941.[16] All three men were reporters when they first came from Cambridge to New York: Stevens for a short time on the *Tribune* (1900—1901), Arensberg as art critic for the *Evening Sun* (during a brief stay in 1905-7), and Sanborn as music critic for the *Globe* (1905-23). Only Pitts Sanborn made his career in journalism, but even so he retained the literary aspirations which the three friends shared (he published one book of poems in 1917, and two novels in 1929 and 1933). It was probably through Sanborn that both Stevens and Arensberg became involved, in 1914, with the group of newspapermen/poets who were responsible for *Trend* and *Rogue* magazines.

The seven or eight years when Arensberg held "open-house" in New York were probably also the years of his longest and closest contact with Stevens. Though he had lived in New York briefly in 1905-7, it was not till he saw the Armory Show in 1913 that Arensberg decided to establish himself there. We can date fairly accurately the period of his New York residence. He and his wife moved to New York in 1914, and they left New York permanently in 1921, to settle in California.[17] A short time before his departure, Arensberg's friendship with Stevens also came to an abrupt end: the two men fought and never spoke to one another again. Stevens described the incident in 1954, in a "confidential" letter to Weldon Kees (*L*, 849-51). Briefly, their final misunderstanding began when Stevens tried to intercede on behalf of a mutual friend who had fallen into

Walter's disfavor: "Walter froze up when I spoke to him and when he froze up, I froze up too.... [We] remained on our high horses. I never saw him again. Shortly after that he left for the coast" (*L,* 850). The New York years which concern us in this essay, then, begin in 1914 and end in 1921. It was during this same time period that Stevens composed most of the poems in *Harmonium.*

The Armory Show appeared in New York from February 18 to March 15, 1913. We may assume that Stevens attended the event, though we have no record of his reactions to it. But he was unequivocal in recalling the Show's effect on Walter Arensberg: "I don't suppose there is anyone to whom the Armory Show of 1913 meant more than it meant to him" (*L,* 821). Arensberg was living in Boston at the time, and had traveled to New York for the occasion. According to the most dramatic version of the story, "Walter visited the exhibition, was transfixed by it, and actually forgot to go home for several days."[18] At the Armory Show Arensberg bought the first of the art works which would comprise his famous collection, and to which he would devote a major part of his life and fortune. Soon after the Armory Show, he and his wife moved to New York, the American center for avant-garde art.

A chief agent in this remarkable conversion was the American painter Walter Pach, who helped to organize the Armory Show. Arensberg and Pach first met at the exhibit, and they were soon spending long hours together discussing the new art.[19] Wallace Stevens recognized the importance of Pach's proselytizing talents: "Probably Pach helped this [the Armory Show] to take the extraordinary hold on him that it took in fact" (*L,* 821). And Stevens, too, came to know Pach well—probably through Arensberg. It was Pach who designed the set for *Bowl, Cat, and Broomstick,* and who illustrated "Earthy Anecdote" and "Moment of Light." And it was most likely through Pach's connection with the Ferrer School that Stevens eventually published two poems and a translation in that school's "house organ," *The Modern School.*[20] Stevens must have known at first hand Pach's persuasive interest in the avant-garde. He certainly admired his enthusiasm, whether or not he shared it entirely, for years later he would remember Walter Pach warmly as "an old friend of mine" (*L,* 490).

What interested Walter Arensberg most at the Armory Show was Cubism. This is evident in the paintings which he collected and displayed in his apartment during the 1910s, and which we can identify from photographs of the Arensbergs' "Main Studio" taken by Charles Sheeler in 1918. Of the thirty-five paintings on the walls, most are Cubist or related to Cubism.[21] Wallace Stevens was attracted to Cubism, too, and his interest was probably nursed during his frequent visits to his friend's apartment.[22] When, in later years, Stevens admitted to "a taste for Braque and a purse for Bombois," he may well have been comparing his own "very small collection" with his memories of the Arensberg salon (*L,* 545).

The Arensberg salon was only one of several literary/artistic centers in New York at the time. Mabel Dodge, Alfred Kreymborg, Lola Ridge, the owners of the Sunwise Turn Bookshop—these and others played host to gatherings of artists and writers.[23] But the most famous center of all was Alfred Stieglitz's Photo-Secession Gallery at 291 Fifth Avenue, and it was "291" which most resembled the Arensberg salon because both emphasized the visual arts. Many of the same guests frequented both places. Charles Sheeler, Charles Demuth, Joseph Stella, Morton Schamberg, Man Ray, Francis Picabia, Marias de Zayas—all these "291" regulars could be found, on occasion, uptown at 33 West 67th Street. Paintings by many of these artists were displayed on Arensberg's walls, and some had even been purchased at "291" exhibits.

So much interaction between these two artistic centers is not surprising. The places devoted to avant-garde art were few in New York in the 1910s, so that the artists were likely to run into each other wherever they chose to gather. But previous studies of the New York avant-garde, from a literary point of view, have overemphasized the similarity between "291" and the Arensberg salon. Both Bram Dijkstra and Dickran Tashjian focus their fine studies almost exclusively on the Stieglitz group and on William Carlos Williams, treating the Arensberg apartment as a minor, uptown annex of "291."[24] But for Wallace Stevens, 33 West 67th Street was the very center of avant-garde activity in New York. It is of the greatest importance for the present study, therefore, to define the distinctive character of the Arensberg salon.

The two "leading actors" in this salon were its host, Arensberg himself, and its artistic center, Marcel Duchamp, whom Arensberg revered. The importance of both these men to the salon as a whole will be considered in detail below. But even if we overlook these two figures, for a moment, the salon retains a particular character which distinguishes it from other literary/artistic centers of the time. It had a "core" of regular members which derived from the mingling of two oddly compatible groups: the *Trend* writers, and the expatriate French artists. This combination was in some ways peculiarly suited to the tastes of Wallace Stevens.

The April, 1914, issue of *Trend* lists Pitts Sanborn as its new Secretary-Treasurer, and in that same issue Walter Arensberg and Carl Van Vechten appear for the first time. Soon Donald Evans, Wallace Stevens, Djuna Barnes, and Allen Norton followed. After the collapse of *Trend,* this same group would found *Rogue* and become "regulars" at the newly established Arensberg salon. Socially fashionable and intellectually witty, this group cultivated a consciously aristocratic air. Their common outlook stemmed in large part from their devotion to Harvard and what it represented: Sanborn, Arensberg, Stevens, and Norton had all attended Harvard. Their "clubbish" attitude was only too clear to those around them, and one's reaction to this phenomenon corresponded inversely to one's democratic sentiments. Alfred Kreymborg, for one, was uncomfortable with this intrusion of Cambridge into New York territory:

> So as not to appear outside the circle, he tried to hold his tea cup nonchalantly and assumed a casual air whenever he was addressed. He even ventured to mimic the languorous speech which, he learned later on, all men acquire at Harvard.[25]

Kreymborg is describing a party at the apartment of Allen and Louise Norton, who were listed in the New York Social Register, and who did not get along well with Alfred Kreymborg. This goes a long way toward explaining Kreymborg's unsympathetic account of the party, which through his eyes appears chillingly formal:

> Clearly, these people respected one another, and their guarded phrases paid tribute accordingly. Thus at least Krimmie, imprisoned in his own aloofness, assured himself.[26]

The breadth of Kreymborg's acquaintance makes his memoir, *Troubadour,* an invaluable record of this period. No other book conveys so well a sense of what life must have been like among the early American modernists. But as a factual record it is unreliable, particularly in respect to Wallace Stevens. According to Louise (Norton) Varèse, for instance, Stevens never attended a party in her apartment, as Kreymborg claims in the above episode; and elsewhere in *Troubadour,* Kreymborg describes another party in the 1910s which included Wallace Stevens and Marianne Moore, though the two poets never met till 1942.[27]

Equally unreliable is Carl Van Vechten, because he is more concerned to be amusing than accurate. But his account of the *Trend* group is certainly closer in spirit to what Stevens must have experienced, as his sympathetic description of Stevens himself suggests:

> Stevens' conversation had been wholly amusing, full of that esoteric banter which may be described as Harvardian, at least generically, but containing some specific elements which made it original in manner as well as in matter.[28]

Van Vechten is concerned to appreciate significant distinctions amid the general "Harvardian" polish. Like Stevens, he clearly flourished in such an atmosphere of shared superiority.

The chief aesthetic inspiration for this group was the English Eighteen-Nineties. The April, 1914, issue of *Trend,* for example, published a poem by Pitts Sanborn entitled, "Salome," and accompanied by an unmistakably Beardsleyesque illustration. *Rogue,* too emulated the *fin de siècle* mood, as Stevens's own poems from this magazine demonstrate. The narrator of "Disillusionment of Ten O'Clock" (*CP,* 66) is a dandy. He naturally applies aesthetic criteria to articles of dress, a mode of discrimination which was particularly at home in *Rogue,* whose regular department, "Philosophical Fashions," deplored the lack of "amusing" menswear: "alas! masculine clothes-reform advances somewhat after the fashion of the Allies...."[29] We may take the title of this poem as a reference to that *locus classicus* of Aestheticism, Whistler's "Ten O'Clock" lecture of 1885.[30] This lecture decries the vulgarization of art—" 'the many' have elbowed 'the few,' and the gentle circle of Art swarms with the intoxicated mob of mediocrity"—but concludes by celebrating the superiority of Art over Nature, and rejoicing in the sovereignty of the Artist, who will continue to thrive even among the Philistines:

> Therefore have we cause to be merry!—and to chase away all care—resolved that all is well—as it ever was.... We have but to wait—until, with the mark of the Gods upon him—there come among us again the chosen—who shall continue what has gone before.[31]

What this lecture describes is, if seen from a less optimistic point of view, the condition of the alienated artist, whose "disillusionment" was more typical of the Nineties aesthete than Whistler's "Ten O'Clock" confidence. Stevens's "Disillusionment of Ten O'Clock" discovers the aesthete in this more dejected mood. Stevens's narrator does not see the imaginative man as "the chosen" with "the mark of the Gods upon him," but as an isolated and peculiar figure. Like so many poets of the Nineties, he longs for a world of exotic beauty (the wildly colored "nightgowns" of his imagination), and laments that such beauty can only be achieved "here and there," and often in very unaesthetic circumstances:

> ... People are not going
> To dream of baboons and periwinkles.
> Only, here and there, an old sailor,
> Drunk and asleep in his boots,
> Catches tigers
> In red weather.

The narrator's rarefied imagination and dandyish pose in this poem; the naughty suggestion of sexuality in "Cy Est Pourtraicte"; and the delicate exoticism of "Tea"—these elements summarize the spirit of the Nineties which survived in *Rogue.*

The spirit of the 1890s had never wholly died in American literary circles. It was kept fresh by the efforts of such as Thomas Bird Mosher, whose *Bibelot* reprinted Nineties verse from 1895 through 1915. It was while reading *Bibelot* that Wallace Stevens encountered the sonnets of David Gray, a discovery which so impressed him that he recorded it in his journal.[32] *Bibelot* ceased publication in 1915; and *Rogue,* which began publication in the same year, may be seen as the final, feverish outburst of an exhausted literary movement. But it is not often recognized that *Rogue* also presages a *new* movement, which would come to be known as New York Dada, and whose principal figures were the Frenchmen who arrived in New York during the brief period when *Rogue* was flourishing, the summer of 1915.

The second series of *Rogue,* published in three oversized issues from October through December of 1916, records a unique mixture of lingering Nineties and proto-Dada elements. These issues are generally overlooked (Hoffman, for instance, does not list them),[33] but they are important to the present study. The October issue includes an item entitled, "**THE** — Eye Test, not a 'Nude Descending a Staircase,'" a piece of carefully contrived nonsense studded with asterisks. A footnote instructs the reader to "replace each * by the word: *the,*" a procedure which clarifies the syntax but not the sense of the paragraph. The clever silliness of this exercise recalls the verbal experiments of Gertrude Stein, who was also published in *Rogue.* But the "Eye Test" was composed and signed by Marcel Duchamp, who was by this time an intimate member of the *Rogue* group, as this announcement in the November, 1916, issue indicates:

> Next to the Russian Ballet the most important event of the season was *Rogue's* Ball on September 29. It was called September Morn because it ended early. Clara Tice was winner of the first costume prize and Marcel Duchamp, one of the judges, was winner of the booby prize...[34]

Duchamp was also the main attraction of the Arensberg salon; he even had a studio adjoining the Arensbergs' apartment.[35]

It was the beginning of World War I that brought Duchamp and other European artists to America. Though the United States did not enter the War until April of 1917, its impact was felt immediately in New York in 1914. In the first place, the lives of many (perhaps most) of Stevens's friends and acquaintances were immediately affected by this catastrophe. Virtually everyone in this "group" had traveled or lived in France (Stevens was the notable exception). Stevens's friends Carl Van Vechten, Pitts Sanborn, and John Covert (Arensberg's cousin) were all in Europe in August, 1914, and recorded their experiences of the mobilization and evacuation.[36] All of these people, including Stevens, spoke French fluently and looked to Paris as the vital center of civilization and art. The German attack on France may have affected this group with an intensity unmatched elsewhere in the United States.

Following this European "invasion," the atmosphere of the Arensberg salon became distinctly French. Other frequent visitors, in addition to Marcel Duchamp, were Francis and Gabrielle Buffet-Picabia, Albert Gleizes and Juliette Roche, Jean and Yvonne Crotti, Henri-Pierre Roche, and Edgar Varèse. French was often spoken in the apartment, and this made some American guests uncomfortable. William Carlos Williams, for one, felt ill-at-ease at the Arensbergs' not only because he did not like Duchamp, but also because, "we weren't, or I wasn't, up to carrying on a witty conversation in French with the latest Parisian arrivals."[37] Others resented what seemed to them the special attention given to these foreigners. "One day one of [Arensberg's] very oldest friends spoke with some soreness to the effect that Walter was giving a lot of time to those Frenchmen and neglecting others," wrote Stevens. But he hastened to add, "I myself had not noticed this" (*L*, 850).

As this addendum suggests, the impact of this invasion on Wallace Stevens was primarily positive. Though he never traveled to Europe, Stevens carried on a long-distance love affair with Paris throughout his life. He must have been very pleased to find the artistic ferment of the French capital suddenly available to him on West 67th Street. And for one who could later assert that "English and French are a single language," and that "one uses French for the pleasure that it gives," the situation provided a rare opportunity to practice the language he loved. He records of a lunch with Arensberg and Duchamp in 1915: "When the three of us spoke French, it sounded like sparrows around a pool of water."[38]

The *Trend/Rogue* group and the French expatriates joined forces in the creation of two short-lived magazines, *Blindman* and *Rongwrong*, both overseen by Marcel Duchamp and published in 1917. Here Duchamp's keen sense for the profoundly disturbing gesture, what we might call his "Dada" sensibility, combined with the more casual humor of the *Rogue* group to form the distinctive attitude known as New York Dada. As William Innes Homer explains:

> If European Dada had a destructive, even self-destructive, character, New York Dada was almost playful. In political terms, the difference was similar to that between the committed revolutionary and the adherent of 'radical chic.'[39]

The headquarters of New York Dada was the Arensberg salon. The rest of this chapter will focus on the two men who best characterize this salon: Marcel Duchamp, its guiding spirit, and Walter Arensberg, its enthusiastic host. The developing interests of these two men provide a suggestive background to the development of Wallace Stevens's *Harmonium*.

That Walter Arensberg was "rather frail in appearance," as Wallace Stevens remembered (*L*, 823), is borne out by the well-known photograph of the *Others* group taken in 1916.[40] Arensberg stands in the back row, arm in arm with Marcel Duchamp. He is wearing a rumpled suit, and if this inattention to dress suggests the distracted scholar, the suggestion is appropriate: "I think that on the whole Walter led a studious life," wrote Stevens (*L*, 822); and it is recorded that Arensberg was sometimes so lost in thought that he became oblivious to his own guests.[41] Arensberg's rounded features give him a youthful appearance corresponding to what Stevens called his "boyish enthusiasm": "He was easily amused," wrote Stevens, "His manner of speech was boyish" (L, 822-23). This enthusiasm was often directed toward intellectual problems—he "very much enjoyed wordy battles over differences of opinion": but he could be equally attracted to personalities. He played host, for example, to the Dolly Sisters, and to a very boisterous Isadora Duncan, and at such times his casual salon gave way to a real party, as Stevens recalled:

> He liked to give parties for people in whom he was interested, although the only one that I recall at the moment is one which was attended by Amy Lowell and Miss Russell. His interest amounted to excitement. (L, 821)

The general impression one gets of Walter Arensberg, then, is of a youthful energy and charm, and an intellectual, even a scholarly, turn of mind. But there was another side of his personality which also affected Wallace Stevens:

> Arensberg always reminded me of the finest vintage champagne: heady, slightly biting, demanding, temperamental, and effervescent. He changed his mind not from day to day, but from hour to hour, so one never knew whether there would be a warm hand clasp or a frigid dismissal.

This impression of Arensberg's changeable nature was recorded by Katherine Kuh who, like Wallace Stevens, eventually had a falling-out with Arensberg and was "banished" from his company.[42] The boyish scholar could also be quick-tempered and slow to forgive.

Such infrequent displays of temper notwithstanding, Arensberg was generally known to be a generous and open-minded host, whose muted role in his own salon contrasted sharply with the role of Stieglitz at "291":

> ... Duchamp's criticism of Stieglitz as a "sort of Socrates," moralizing and humorless, must be seen as an unfavorable comparison to his preferred host, the less doctrinaire Arensberg. While the 291 group was essentially an extension of Stieglitz and his thought, the freedom of the Arensberg circle was much more in keeping with the development of Dada.[43]

One might add that the freer atmosphere of the Arensberg salon was also better suited to the independent mind of Wallace Stevens.

Walter Arensberg's chief passion was modern art, but he had other important interests, and two of these have some special bearing on the present study: chess and cryptography. Arensberg was a member of the Harvard Chess Club, and his interest in the game continued in New York, as Stevens remembered: "Walter used to like to play chess and frequently went to the New York Chess Club with Duchamp" (L, 823). Duchamp's interest in chess may even have surpassed Arensberg's: in later years the Frenchman gave up art altogether, devoted most of his time to chess, and became an international chess champion. The Arensberg salon naturally reflected the common obsession of these two friends. Displayed on the walls were Duchamp's *Chess Players* (1911) and *King and Queen Surrounded by Swift Nudes* (1912). Chess motifs also appeared in the little magazines associated with the salon: *Rogue* had a chessboard-like cover, for instance, and *Rongwrong* printed the plan of a game between Picabia "for *391*" and Henri-Pierre Roche "for *Blindman*." Stevens himself probably played chess occasionally. (We have no record of his doing so, but his daughter, Holly, remembers being given a chess set once as a girl.)[44] Other chess enthusiasts among Arensberg's frequent guests were Elmer Ernest Southard (another Harvard friend), Man Ray, Allen Norton, and Alfred Kreymborg.

Chess is a war game. To play it regularly for amusement while a real war ravaged Europe was heavily ironic, an observation that could scarcely have escaped the attention of the concerned Arensberg circle. Wallace Stevens, at least, seems to have brooded over this curious circumstance, for later—during another war—his imagination proposed a very similar situation as a metaphor for his own poetry:

> ... if one happened to be playing checkers under the Maginot Line, subject to a call at any moment to do some job that might be one's last job, one would spend a good deal of time thinking in order to make the situation seem reasonable, inevitable, and free from question.
> I suppose that, in the last analysis, my own main objective is to do that kind of thinking...
> (*L*, 346)

Stevens conceives of his own poetic activity as the playing of a board game under the immediate pressure of war. This is a unique metaphor for his poetry. More usually, during World War II, Stevens would speak of the poet as a soldier, and of poetic activity as combat. Here, instead, in searching for an analogy to suggest the "kind of thinking" he hopes to achieve in his writing, he has perhaps recalled the experience of his own poetic growth, under the cloud of World War I, among the chess-playing refugees of the Arensberg salon.

Arensberg's interest in chess was characteristically cerebral. "Walter was a great chess player," recalls William M. Ivins, Jr., "one of the kind that plays while taking a walk in the country, calling the moves, but no board...."[45] That Arensberg was interested primarily by the abstract problems the game presented is confirmed in Alfred Kreymborg's account of his first meeting with the art collector:

> ... [Krimmie] found himself sitting near Arensberg and humored his neighbor's whim for talking chess. The latter was concerned with the theories of the game, rather than with contests over the board...[46]

Like Arensberg, Wallace Stevens was also interested in "theory" at this time—his poem of this title, his three plays, and his series of "anecdotes" are sufficient illustration of this interest. But the two friends probably did not agree quite so readily on aesthetic matters as this coincidence might suggest. Stevens's comment, for instance, that "Earthy Anecdote" (1918) had "a good deal of theory about it" (*L*, 204), might seem to admit an aesthetic program neatly conforming to Arensberg's taste for abstraction. But about Walter Pach's illustration for the same poem, in the same year, Stevens wrote: "[it] is just the opposite of my idea. I intended something quite concrete: actual animals, not original chaos" (*L*, 209). Whatever Stevens's approach to chess may have been, where poetry was concerned he preferred to play with the board and pieces.

For Walter Arensberg, intellectual interest was closely allied with aesthetic response. Kreymborg's account of their first meeting continues: "[Walter] divulged a temperament so susceptible to [chess's] aesthetic and philosophical aspects that Krimmie responded cordially."[47] Arensberg's aesthetic appreciation of intellectual problems, which impressed Kreymborg in regard to chess, also characterized his love of modern art:

> For him it sometimes seemed as though pictures were interesting just to the extent that they set him intellectual and psychological problems to speculate about—almost as though they were very complicated chess problems.[48]

It is probably this trait Stevens had in mind when he wrote of Arensberg that, "He was just the man to become absorbed in cubism and in everything that followed" (*L*, 822). And this same turn of mind may explain another of Arensberg's life-long enthusiasms, the literary use of cryptography.

Walter Arensberg was interested in cryptography at least as early as his Harvard days, when one of his friends, a man named William Stone Booth, was trying to prove through cryptographic readings that Shakespeare was Bacon.[49] This same pursuit was to engage Arensberg for the rest of his life: "He must have spent years on his own particular Baconian theory," wrote Stevens (*L*, 822), and his extended research resulted in six books.[50] During his New York years in particular, Arensberg was at work on two books: *The Cryptography of Dante* (1921) and *The Cryptography of Shakespeare* (1922). Cryptography must have been discussed regularly at his salon, and it certainly caught the interest of some of his guests, for cryptographic elements appear in the work of artists associated with the Arensberg circle during this period—Man Ray, Marcel Duchamp, Katherine Dreier, and John Covert among them.[51]

Cryptography was the germ of Arensberg's particular aesthetic theory. He describes the motive behind the literary use of cryptography as

> the desire... to express and solve, if solving be possible, the problem of appearance and reality.... [the duplicities of cryptographic literature] are a literal expression, a parallel, of

the duplicities of the world in which we live; they are intended, in their deepest aspects, to express the difference between what things *are* and what things *seem.*[52]

Arensberg is making very large claims for what is ordinarily considered a rather specialized form of intellectual amusement. He is stating a theory of art which is also a theory of life: a cryptogram becomes, for him, the type for a particular kind of art, whose confusing surface masks a deeper, but elusive, truth. This kind of art is a deliberate imitation of the way we live our lives, having to work our way through the daily chaos to some more orderly vision of meaning. This aesthetic theory describes fairly well the art of Marcel Duchamp, which we shall consider shortly. It also suggests a very basic sympathy between Walter Arensberg and Wallace Stevens. If we should substitute "imagination and reality" for "appearance and reality" in the above quotation, we would hardly be able to distinguish its point of view from the later aesthetic theories of Stevens (which were grounded, like the theories of most poets, in his own earlier practice).

Stevens's poetry might be termed "cryptic," in a general way, simply because it is difficult. "Poetry must resist the intelligence almost successfully," he would write in the "Adagia," asserting—like Arensberg—that to conceal meaning is part of the artist's task.[53] In those poems we think of as most characteristic of *Harmonium*—"Le Monocle de Mon Oncle," "Bantams in Pine-Woods," "The Emperor of Ice-Cream," etc.—this concealment is achieved through Stevens's uniquely flamboyant style. The poem's "cryptic" surface masks its meaning so effectively that certain of Stevens's critics have thought he was writing gorgeous nonsense verse. To search out the meaning in such poetry requires concentrated and prolonged attention. This is precisely what Walter Conrad Arensberg expected of all art, as Stevens distinctly recalled: "He told me once of having looked steadily at a piece of sculpture in one of the large museums for three hours. He did a thing of that kind in the hope of some extraordinary disclosure coming to him" (*L,* 823). As poet and reader, Stevens and Arensberg were unusually well suited to each other.

It is perhaps not so surprising, then, to find Stevens echoing in his poetry Arensberg's cryptographic interests. In the introductory chapter to *The Cryptography of Dante* (1921), Arensberg outlines his cryptographic theories, using examples which must have been repeated often at his salon during the preceding years. Here is one, illustrating the point that cryptography may be used to "derive the *form* of the work from the idea it expresses":

> For the mystic or the symbolist of the past a word had a closer relation with the thing which it names.... An example of this conception appears, indeed, in the fancy, to which Dante himself alludes, that the form of the Italian word *omo,* "man," is written in the human face, the two o's represented by the eyes, the M represented by the line of the nose and the outlines of the cheeks.[54]

So fanciful an approach to etymology suggested humorous poetic possibilities to Wallace Stevens. His manuscript poem, "Headache," begins with Arensberg's example, but uses it to make a satiric point about poetry and about life. The poem begins:

> The letters of the alphabet
> Are representative of parts of the head.
> Ears are gs
> Ls are the edges of the teeth
> Ms are the wrinkled skin between the eyes
> In frowns.
> The nostrils and the bridge of the nose
> Are ps or bs.
> The mouth is o.
> There are letters in the hair.

Thus far the poem has the same structure as Stevens's "Theory" (1917), which begins with the thesis, "I am what is around me," and then lists examples to support the assertion. "Headache" is relatively straightforward up to this point: The alphabet is a set of abstract symbols derived from the parts of the human head—or, to drop the metaphor, a set of symbols abstracted from our experience of the world. The reader's difficulties occur in the second half of the poem, when Stevens suddenly leaps into bizarre satire:

> [The alphabet is a collection
> Of satirical design.]
> Worms frown... [They] are full of mouths,
> [They] bite, twitch their ears...
> [They lure.]
> The maker of the alphabet
> Had a headache.[55]

The trouble with abstract symbols (the poem says) is that immediately they are imagined, they begin to take on a life of their own; they become "worms" in the shape of letters, their intransigence reminding us always of the distance between our most earnest abstractions and the things they are meant to represent. The message conveyed by these "worms" turns out to be sheer nonsense: if we decipher their movements in the order they are recorded in lines thirteen and fourteen, they read "MOLG." Despite this failure to find meaning, however, the worms still "lure"—we are still inclined to create abstractions in order to make sense of things.

The concept of this poem is interesting, if weird, but Stevens was unable to find language which could support the wrenching transition between its two halves. His difficulty is recorded in the numerous corrections on the manuscript. He intended the "worms" to embody three different metaphorical senses: they are the lines which form the individual letters (13-14); they are fishing-worms which "lure" (15); and they are symbols of death, as in "The Worms at Heaven's Gate." (This last sense is appropriate because it is chiefly the idea of death that frustrates man's comprehension.) Stevens could not find a way of clarifying this intention without throwing too much emphasis on what is only a subsidiary image in the poem. In the end, the poem remained unpublished.

"Headache" also repays comparison with Ezra Pound's "Dogmatic Statement Concerning the Game of Chess: Theme for a Series of Pictures" (1915), as A. Walton Litz has pointed out. Both poems employ abstract signs "to elimate rhetorical formulas through a language of precise form."[56] That this poem can maintain friendly relations with both chess and cryptographt perhaps serves to illustrate the compatibility of Stevens's and Arensberg's aesthetic interests at this time.

Chief among Walter Arensberg's contagious enthusiasms was the art of Marcel Duchamp. As one critic has put it, "Duchamp was the spark plug that ignited him."[57] Though the French artist did not visit the United States till 1915, when he moved to New York to escape the War, his name was already familiar here before his arrival. His painting, *Nude Descending a Staircase*, had caused a furor at the Armory Show in 1913, and was to remain a symbol for years afterwards, in the American press, of all modern tendencies in art. Duchamp clearly had a genius for challenging complacent, bourgeois assumptions about the nature of art, and this talent appealed strongly to the recent and fervent "convert" to modernism, Walter Arensberg.

It is perhaps difficult from this distance to see why the *Nude* should have been so shocking to American tastes. One reason, of course, was its manner of execution. Duchamp's stylistic blend of Cubism (the figure's body was suggested by an arrangement of flesh-colored geometrical planes) and Futurism (it emphasized the kinetic motion of the figure) seemed a slap in the face of the entire Western tradition of representational art. But Man Ray is surely right in locating the principal public offense in the painting's title: "If the picture, 'Nude Descending a Staircase,' had not had that title, it would never have attracted any attention at all. It was the title. Let's face it."[58]

Odd titles, which seem at first to bear only a tangential relation to the works they adorn, have become so accepted that we may overlook the fact that Duchamp was a pioneer in this respect. Odd titles were even "old hat" in art circles as early as 1917, when a reviewer of the first Independents Exhibition complained that the works displayed "make the usual impression of absolute incongruity between the title and picture."[59] But when Duchamp first tried to exhibit the *Nude,* at the Paris Independents Exhibition of 1912, it was withdrawn from the show after Albert Gleizes's request "at least to change the title."[60] Duchamp had begun experimenting with the significant interplay between a work of art and its title in 1911, after which time, he writes, "I always gave an important role to the title, which I added and treated like an invisible color."[61] The title became an integral part of the art work: he even went so far as to engrave the title on some of his "readymades." A "whimsical obliqueness" (the phrase is Milton Brown's) characterized Duchamp's titles, "which were essential elements of the esthetic idea."[62] In the case of the *Nude*, the title is "oblique" because the naked female anatomy is barely recognizable in the geometrical patterns of the painting; and it is "whimsical" because it arouses titillating expectations which the painting itself frustrates. The phrase "whimsical obliqueness" applies equally well to many of Wallace Stevens's most characteristic titles: "The Man Whose Pharynx Was Bad," "Tea at the Palaz of Hoon," "Le Monocle de Mon Oncle," are only a few of the most obvious examples from *Harmonium*. Stevens, like Duchamp, placed great importance on titles: "Very often the title occurs to me before anything else occurs to me"; and he sometimes worried that their "obliqueness" was too pronounced: "Possibly the relation [between the titles and the poems] is not as direct and as literal as it ought to be."[63]

The title, "Nude Descending a Staircase," was deliberately indecorous. At the time, a painted nude was expected to be reclining, motionless, with the private portions of her anatomy carefully concealed. Duchamp's nude, on the contrary, stood upright and shamelessly walked downstairs. The idea of a nude in motion appealed to Duchamp, for he completed in the same year, 1912, *King and Queen Surrounded by Swift Nudes*, which, together with a copy of the *Nude Descending a Staircase*, hung in Arensberg's apartment throughout the 1910s. Stevens must have responded to this motif, for he employed it in his poem of 1919, "The Paltry Nude Starts on a Spring Voyage." But the aesthetic affinities of these two men extend deeper than their similar titles. Duchamp explains the conception of *King and Queen Surrounded by Swift Nudes* as follows:

> The title, "King and Queen," was... taken from chess but the players... have been eliminated and replaced by the chess figures of the king and queen. The swift nudes are a flight of imagination introduced to satisfy my preoccupation of movement still present in this painting.... It is a theme of motion in a frame of static entities. In other words the static entities are represented by the king and queen, while the swift nudes are based on the theme of motion.[64]

The interplay of imagination and reality, figured in an aesthetic treatment of motion and stasis, is also one of the principal themes of *Harmonium*. As Joseph Riddel has written, apropos of "Domination of Black":

> This tension between the still self and the turning world... provides the major oppositions of Stevens' early poetry, which comes to discover, as in "Fabliau of Florida"(*CP*, 23), that if the imagination can bear one enchantingly "outward into heaven," there will, nonetheless, "never be an end/ To this droning of the surf."[65]

When Duchamp first arrived in New York on June 15, 1915, he was taken immediately to the apartment of Walter Arensberg, to whom he had an introduction through their mutual friend, Walter Pach. Duchamp and Arensberg became friendly at once, and Duchamp occupied the Arensbergs' apartment that summer while they were out of town. Some time later, Duchamp was occupying his own studio which adjoined the Arensberg apartment.[66]

Stevens met Duchamp not long after his arrival in the United States. He wrote to his wife on August 3, 1915:

> Walter Arensberg telephoned yesterday afternoon and asked me to take dinner with him at the Brevoort with Marcel Duchamp, the man who painted *The Nude Descending A Staircase*.... After dinner, we went up to Arensberg's apartment and looked at some of Duchamp's things. I made very little out of them. But naturally, without sophistication in that direction, and with only very rudimentary feeling about art, I expect little of myself....[67]

Stevens's confession here that he "made very little of" Duchamp's work has been taken to indicate that "he did not share Arensberg's enthusiasm for Duchamp's 'Nude Descending a Staircase'..."[68] But this is surely a misreading of Stevens's letter. Even if he did not "understand" Duchamp's work at this early date (and his comments need not refer, in this particular instance, to the already famous *Nude*), it would be most unlike Stevens to admit lack of sophistication in artistic matters without aspiring to correct his own inadequacy in this regard. If finally the *Nude* did not please him, it is not because he and Duchamp lacked any common aesthetic interests. I have already suggested above that their central artistic preoccupations sometimes coincide strikingly. And the incidental parallels between their careers in the 1910s make the prospect of a comparative study all the more intriguing. Duchamp lived in New York between 1915 and 1923, the very years during which Stevens was writing *Harmonium*.[69] And when Duchamp departed for Europe in 1923, he abandoned painting entirely (a renunciation legendary in the art world). So Stevens, after the publication of *Harmonium* in 1923, appears to have stopped writing entirely for nearly six years.

A convenient introduction to Duchamp's art is provided in the second (and last) issue of his Dada publication, *The Blindman*. This magazine was founded as the official organ of the Society of Independent Artists, which was conceived and organized in the Arensberg apartment, and which held its First Annual Exhibition at the Grand Central Palace on April 10, 1917, four days after the United States entered World War I. The second issue of *Blindman* discussed this exhibition, and we know that Stevens read it: Pitts Sanborn sent him a copy on May 23, 1917.[70]

The cover of *Blindman,* Number 2, is a reproduction of Duchamp's *Chocolate Grinder* (1914). This mechanical representation is part of

Duchamp's effort to "get out of the Cubist straitjacket,"[71] and it reappears as a motif in the "Bachelors" section of Duchamp's masterpiece, the *Large Glass* (a.k.a. *The Bride Stripped Bare by Her Bachelors, Even*), which would be left finally uncompleted in 1923. Duchamp was one of the first painters to treat the machine as a suitable subject. Others in New York who were exploring the possibilities of mechanical imagery were Morton Schamberg, two of whose *Mechanical Abstractions* were displayed in the Arensberg apartment, and Francis Picabia, whose mechanical "portraits" had appeared in Stieglitz's *291*.[72] While Futurism was glorifying the machine, these New York artists—especially Duchamp and Picabia—treated machinery with humor. Picabia's *Portrait d'une Jeune Fille Americaine dans l'Etat de Nudite,* for instance, is a drawing of a spark plug, a none-too-subtle reference to the girl's stimulating effect on the artist. Duchamp's "mechanomorphic" paintings, like his *Bride* of 1912 (which also reappeared in the *Large Glass*), depicted the human body as a composite of machine-like parts.

As should be clear from the few illustrations cited above, the mechanomorphic imagery employed by these artists usually embodies a sexual theme. Duchamp's *Large Glass* is a statement of sexual frustration, in which both the Bride and her Bachelors, isolated from each other in their separate domains, are represented by mechanical imagery.[73] And the *Chocolate Grinder* is an autoerotic motif, alluding to the French saying, "The bachelor grinds his chocolate by himself."[74] By placing the *Chocolate Grinder* on the cover of *Blindman,* Duchamp is protesting the rejection of his entry, the famous *Fountain,* from the Independents Exhibition which was to have no jury; the image questions the sincerity of the hanging committee's professed commitment to uninhibited artistic creativity.

Wallace Stevens explored the poetic possibilities of such humorous machine imagery in one of his least successful poems, "Romance for a Demoiselle Lying in the Grass." The argument of the poem tries to achieve a deadpan humor like that of Duchamp or Picabia: human sexuality in its purely sexual aspect is a model of simplicity, the speaker says. It is not subject to change, it is a "given"—it is "monotonous."

> It is grass.
> It is monotonous.
>
> The monotony
> Is like your port which conceals
> All your characters
> And their desires. . . .

If this is true of sex, why should not love partake of the same absolute existence? Why not take this solid principle, the mechanical operation of physical desire, and apply it as a paradigm in the spiritual realm?

I might make many images of this
And twang nobler notes
Of larger sentiment.

But I invoke the monotony of monotonies
Free from images and change.

Why should I savor love
With tragedy and comedy?

Clasp me,
Delicatest machine.

The irony of the situation is that the speaker's transcendental longings have led him not to transcend but to become even more entangled in the appealing but traitorous simplicity of the merely physical. Unfortunately the poem does not quite work: the usual meaning of "monotony," that of boring repetition, immediately undercuts the speaker's intended sense of "absolute," so that the sophistry of his argument is more apparent than the ingenuity of Stevens's conceit.

A more successful treatment of the same theme is the eleventh stanza of "Le Monocle de Mon Oncle." This poem replies to the attitude expressed in "Romance for a Demoiselle..." and again mixes sexual with mechanistic imagery:

If sex were all, then every trembling hand
Could make us squeak, like dolls, the wished-for words.
But note the unconscionable treachery of fate,
That makes us weep, laugh, grunt and groan, and shout
Doleful heroics, pinching gestures forth
From madness or delight, without regard
To that first, foremost law. Anguishing hour!

In an earlier age the poet might have compared man's sensual appetites to those of beasts. Stevens wished to avoid the suggestion of a divinely-ordered hierarchy which that comparison might imply, and preferred a colder, more modern comparison. Men who overvalue sex do not become like beasts, but like machines—they become "dolls." Stevens is debunking sex, but not on moral grounds—his very explicitness proves that. The system of values proposed here is not based on standard moral rectitude, but on degrees of "aliveness," so that the mechanomorphic imagery of the dolls conveys the very essence of his poetic statement.

The main feature of *Blindman 2* is introduced, on page four, by a full-page photograph of Duchamp's "readymade" entitled, *Fountain by R. Mutt.* The caption reads, "The Exhibit Refused by the Independents," and the picture shows an ordinary porcelain urinal. *Fountain* is the most famous of

Duchamp's "readymades," an art form he invented in 1913, though the term "readymade" was not coined until 1915. Duchamp's first readymade, *Bicycle Wheel,* consisted of a bicycle wheel mounted upside-down on top of a four-legged stool. Over the next decade the artist created a number of these works. In each of them an ordinary mass-produced object—e.g., a bottlerack, a snowshovel, a hatrack—is displayed as an art object, often without alteration except for the addition of a title. The concept of a readymade naturally raises the most fundamental aesthetic questions. The viewer's initially puzzled query, "Is it art?", must soon lead to the complex philosophical issue, "*What* is art?" As Duchamp admitted years later, "I was interested in ideas—not merely in visual products. I wanted to put [art] once again at the service of the mind."[75] In acknowledgment of this purpose in Duchamp's art, one critic has labeled him "the twentieth century's most cerebral artist."[76]

Fountain calls into question, among other things, the traditional role of the artist as craftsman. This point is addressed by Louise Norton in *Blindman 2:*

> To those who say that Mr. Mutt's exhibit may be Art, but is it the art of Mr. Mutt since a plumber made it? I reply simply that the Fountain was not made by a plumber but by the force of an imagination....[77]

It is the concept of the readymade, and not the object itself, which is of primary aesthetic interest. In the same issue of *Blindman* the article, "The Richard Mutt Case," is even more explicit on this point, defining the artist not as a craftsman, but simply as one who chooses:

> Whether Mr. Mutt with his own hands made the fountain or not has no importance. He CHOSE it. He took an ordinary ariticle of life, placed it so that its useful significance disappeared under the new title and point of view—created a new thought for that object.[78]

According to both these quotations it is not the execution but the *idea* behind the work which makes the readymade interesting. Emphasis is thrown upon the object itself, placed in a strange environment and divorced from its practical function so that it is viewed solely as a "thing" without relation to its use. And equal emphasis is placed upon the artist, not as craftsman, but as gifted perceiver whose *choice* of an object is seen as a creative act. The readymade thus becomes the focus of a meditation on the relation between external things and our perception of them, or—to use the terms Wallace Stevens would later employ to describe the same effect in his own poetry—a self-conscious meditation on the relation between reality and imagination.

To what degree do external things exist separate from our perceptions of them? To what degree do our perceptions alter the things perceived, and vice versa? Stevens posed these epistemological questions in a variety of ways during the 1910s: as philosophical postulates ("I am what is around me"; "The soul, he said, is composed/ Of the external world"); as interactions between mind and landscape (the "Primordia" series); as deliberate manipulations of perceptual apparatus (e.g., *Carlos among the Candles*), etc. For Stevens, as for Duchamp, the artist's role is defined in terms of these questions, so that it is not surprising to discover that one of *Harmonium's* best-known poems on this subject—"Anecdote of the Jar" (*CP,* 76)—bears a close family resemblance to Duchamp's readymades. The enigmatic gesture which is the subject of this poem might well describe the creation of a readymade. The speaker (the artist, or poet) selects an ordinary object, and places it in a strange context: "I *placed* a jar in Tennessee,/ And round it was, upon a hill." In doing so he "creates a new thought for that object," as *Blindman* said of Duchamp's "Fountain," so that the new arrangement is something unique: "Like nothing else in Tennessee."

Characteristic of both "Anecdote of the Jar" and Duchamp's *Fountain* is an essential ambiguity. To place a jar on a hill in Tennessee, and to place a porcelain urinal on its side atop a pedestal, are both ambiguous (as well as bizarre) gestures. In each case the nature of the object itself is also ambiguous: Is it to be considered as a machine-made object, without aesthetic value in itself, an instance of anti-art? Or is it to be considered a worthy example of utilitarian design? It is the nature of a readymade to inspire these questions without resolving them. Duchamp's "Bottlerack" (1914), for instance, mass-produced in dull metal, is unquestionably "gray and bare," like Stevens's jar; but it has also been praised as "a more beautiful form than almost anything made, in 1914, as sculpture."[79] In the same way, Stevens's jar has been endlessly discussed as an "artifact," but whether its significance as such in the poem is negative or positive is the subject of a critical controversy which testifies to its essential ambiguity. "One of the essentials of poetry is ambiguity," wrote Stevens, "I don't feel that I have touched the thing until I touch it in ambiguous form."[80]

In order to define more precisely what this particular "anecdote" has in common with Duchamp's readymades, it may be helpful to contrast it with another "readymade-like" poem. William Carlos Williams also knew Duchamp, and described his readymades in the "Prologue" to *Kora in Hell* (1918):

> One day Duchamp decided that his composition for that day would be the first thing that struck his eye in the first hardware store he should enter. It turned out to be a pickaxe which he bought and set up in his studio. This was his composition.[81]

Williams's own "Red Wheelbarrow" answers well enough to this same description:

> so much depends
> upon

a red wheel
barrow

glazed with rain
water

beside the white
chickens[82]

As Dickran Tashjian has pointed out, this poem "seizes the particular experience as a readymade...." But Williams's straightforward, deadpan presentation of the wheelbarrow contrasts revealingly with Stevens's more elaborate evocation of the jar. Williams attempts to be entirely objective, to exclude all emotive or interpretive language in the interests of presenting "the wheelbarrow itself, the readymade transposed into language through accurate, concise description and subtle phrasing."[83] Stevens, on the other hand, is as much concerned—in "Anecdote of the Jar"—with ideas about the thing as with the thing itself. Instead of trying to achieve the plainly objective voice of William's poem, Stevens adopts his characteristic persona (the "I" of his poem) of a dandy. The speaker of "Anecdote of the Jar" is fastidiously concerned that the object of his present attention achieve a certain aesthetic harmony with its surroundings. His discriminating sensibility perceives the wilderness as "slovenly," and though he admits that the jar does not entirely meet his exacting standards (it is unprepossessingly "gray and bare"), he notes with satisfaction that in its tasteful placement it appears to advantage as "tall" and "of a port in air." (The meaning of this last phrase may be ambiguous, but its diction is unmistakably elevated.)

It is precisely this difference in temperament between the two poets that Williams points out later in the "Prologue" to *Kora in Hell,* just before quoting at length from one of Stevens's letters to him:

The true value is that peculiarity which gives an object a character by itself. The associational or sentimental value is the false. Its imposition is due to lack of imagination, to an easy lateral sliding.... Here I clash with Wallace Stevens.[84]

What Williams refers to disparagingly as "the associational or sentimental value" is, to adopt the vocabulary which Williams deliberately avoids, the traditional domain of taste and sensibility. The task of the modern American poet meant, for Williams, expunging every trace of the twilight sentiment and facile phrasing of his own *Poems* (1909). Stevens, too, avidly sought the "new," but in creating his own poetic voice he transmuted elements borrowed from the Nineties dandy and aesthete. Here he parted company with his friend, Williams.

The speaker in "Anecdote of the Jar" is a man of taste, and the central irony of the poem rests in the application of so refined a point of view to the distinctly unrefined example of a jar on a hill. The determining personality of the artist (or his persona) is, to a great extent, the major interest of the poem. The same is true of Duchamp's readymades. The very concept of the readymade pushes the cult of "taste" to its furthest extreme: amid the deliberate ambiguities of such an artistic gesture, all that can be asserted with any assurance is the sovereignty and intellectual interest of the artist's choice.

Duchamp himself is "generally described as a modern dandy in appearance and temperament,"[85] and in this respect he has more in common with Wallace Stevens than with William Carlos Williams. Both Duchamp and Stevens adopted the pose of the dandy in their work, and developed it into a new and distinct artistic "voice." Both *Fountain* and "Anecdote of the Jar" assume the trappings of the Nineties cult of sensibility in order to dramatize, instead, the enigmatic authority of the modern artist. Ironically, it is this common link with tradition which most closely connects these two most modern artists.

This combination of *fin de siècle* and modernist impulses is, as we have noted, characteristic of the Arensberg salon generally. A lingering Nineties sensibility, in the person of the *Trend/Rogue* writers, and the proto-Dada tendencies of the French expatriates, combined to produce the phenomenon known as New York Dada. These same elements also contributed to the gradual emergence, during the 1910s, of the mature poetic style of Wallace Stevens. The atmosphere of the salon—aristocratic, playful, intellectual, with a French accent and above all a consuming interest in art—this atmosphere corresponds strikingly to the spirit of *Harmonium*. It is reasonable to suppose, then, that when Stevens wrote (in 1922) that he had "got far away from the art crowd," he was confessing as well a growing estrangement, in his own life, from the concerns which had characterized this early phase of his poetic career. Family and business responsibilities increasingly directed Stevens's attention away from New York; and his final break with Walter Arensberg propelled him further in this direction. Arensberg left New York for California in 1921. On August 24, 1922, Stevens wrote to Harriet Monroe: "I . . . saw Marcel Duchamp in New York recently. He seemed like a cat that had been left behind" (*L*, 228). The sense of abandonment Stevens attributes to Duchamp here perhaps reflects his own feelings about the double loss of a close friend and the stimulus of "the art crowd." In hindsight we can also see that this mood forebodes the imminent departure of Stevens's Muse. Soon after the publication of *Harmonium* in 1923, Stevens lapsed into poetic silence, and apparently did not resume writing again until 1930. The dissolution of the Arensberg group serves as a convenient and suggestive metaphor for the abrupt ending of Stevens's *Harmonium* period.

Part II

Some Figures Behind *Harmonium*

3

Walter Conrad Arensberg

Thus far I have tried to show the poet of *Harmonium* in his immediate social and artistic context, as one member of the groups I have called the "Patagonians" and the "art crowd." Stevens's imaginative engagement with these groups, evident in his poetry of the time, significantly qualifies his legendary reputation as an isolated and solitary figure. But perhaps even more damaging to this legend is the fact that Stevens also, in these early years, worked closely and *directly* with other poets: exchanging criticism, sharing themes—and even, in one case, agreeing to collaborate on a book of poems. His literary relationships with Walter Conrad Arensberg, Donald Evans, William Carlos Williams, and the French soldier/poet named Eugène Emmanuel Lemercier, were close enough that we might, without greatly exaggerating, call them all "collaborations."

The first of these "collaborators," Walter Arensberg, we have already seen as cryptographer, chess enthusiast, and art collector. He was also an accomplished poet. At Harvard he had been elected Class Poet (1900), and—unlike Stevens—had continued writing poems after graduation. His first book, *Poems* (1914), contained formally expert poems deriving from the French Symbolists and the English Eighteen-Nineties.[1] This dual emphasis was typical of the early poetry of most of the avant-garde poets, and it anticipated the character of his future "salon". His first poems after his move to New York (published in *Trend* between April 1914 and January 1915) continued in the same manner. But with the appearance of *Others*, of which he was co-founder (with Alfred Kreymborg) in 1915, he began writing free verse. Perhaps the best example of Arensberg's style is "Voyage à L'Infini," first published in *Others* (September 1915) and often cited for its tantalizing parallels to Stevens's "Sunday Morning":[2]

VOYAGE À L'INFINI

The swan existing
Is like a song with an accompaniment
Imaginary.

Across the glassy lake,
Across the lake to the shadow of the willows,
It is accompanied by an image,
—As by Debussy's
"Reflets dans l'eau."

The swan that is
Reflects
Upon the solitary water—breast to breast
With the duplicity:
"The other one !"

And breast to breast it is confused.
O visionary wedding! O stateliness of the
 procession!
It is accompanied by the image of itself
Alone.

At night
The lake is a wide silence,
Without imagination.

Those final lines are surely related to Stevens's "wide water, without sound," though we do not know whose poem was written first. In any case, "Voyage à L'Infini" is a remarkable poem. The "duplicity" of the swan and its reflection figures the interdependence of imagination and reality, a theme which absorbed both Arensberg and Stevens. And the counterpoint between the musical analogies (the repeated pun in "accompaniment," the reference to Debussy's piano piece) and the visual image creates a sense of rippling, expanding correspondences. This sense, together with the poem's emphasis on mood, its variations of a single visual image, its rhythmic repetition of words, and its general "musical" quality—all this makes "Voyage à L'Infini" much like Stevens's own "Domination of Black," for example. Arensberg's poem would probably not seem out of place in *Harmonium*.

"Voyage à L'Infini" appeared in *Idols* (1916), Arensberg's last book of poems. But Arensberg did not, as critics generally assume, stop writing poetry immediately with the publication of this book. Between 1916 and 1919 he published several pieces best described as "Dada" poems in the Dada magazines *Rogue, Blind Man, 391,* and *TNT*.[3] These poems are bizarre and obscure. Perhaps they represent the logical poetic extreme of Arensberg's involvement with New York Dada; or perhaps his interest in poetry simply flagged. Whatever the explanation, after 1919 Arensberg directed all his literary energy to the Bacon/Shakespeare controversy.

But it is the poet of "Voyage à L'Infini" who most resembles Wallace Stevens. When Stevens later wrote his own poem about a swan, and about the relation between imagination and reality, he may have remembered this and sought Arensberg's advice. "Sonatina to Hans Christian" uses Hans Christian Anderson's tale of the "ugly duckling" as a metaphor for the "duplicity"of our world. A recently discovered manuscript, in Stevens's handwriting, has an early version of this poem on the left side of the page, and an alternate version headed "WCA suggests" on the right. Both of these are included below, together with the final lines of the published version (*CP,* 109):

SONATINA TO HANS CHRISTIAN

Manuscript Version

1 If any duck in any brook,
2 Fluttering the water
3 For your crumb,
4 Seemed the helpless daughter

5 Of a mother
6 Regretful that she bore her;
7 Or of another,
8 *Full of first longing for her;

9   What of the dove
10 *Or lark, or any bird one sees?
11 *What of the very trees,
12 And intonations of the trees?

13 *What of the light
14 That lights and dims the stars?
15 Do you know, Hans Christian
16 *Now that you know the night?

"WCA Suggests"

8 *Barren, and longing for her;

  What of the dove,
10 *Or thrush, or any singing mysteries?
11 *What of the tones
  And intonations of the trees?

13 *What of the might
  That lights and dims the stars?
  Do you know, Hans Christian,
16 *Now that you see the night?

Final Version

8 *Barren and longing for her;

  What of the dove,
10 *Or thrush, or any singing mysteries?
11 *What of the trees
  And intonations of the trees?

13 *What of the night
  That lights and dims the stars?
  Do you know, Hans Christian,
16 *Now that you see the night?

Though Stevens did not adopt all of Arensberg's revisions, the two poets clearly agreed about what was wrong with the original poem: they both revised the same five lines. Some of Arensberg's suggestions were primarily stylistic.

He changed repeated words, for instance ("trees" to "tones," line 11; "light" to "might," 13; "know" to "see," 16). Stevens, however, may have been using repetition deliberately (emphasizing the "duality" of his theme), for he reinstated two repetitions in his final version ("trees," 11; "night," 13). And however one judges the relative harmonic values of variation and repetition in this case, the *sense* of Stevens's final version is more effective.

But the revisions Arensberg suggested in lines 8 and 10 are more substantial, and Stevens did adopt these. The chief aim of these changes is to sharpen the poem's meaning. In his second stanza, Stevens intended to contrast the two "mothers" of the ugly duckling. These represent, in Ronald Sukenick's formulation, "The first 'mother': hostile nature; the second: the chaos to which all must return."[5] They are the attendant spirits, respectively, of birth and death, so that the metamorphosis of the ugly duckling into a beautiful swan under such malign influences is simply another figure for Stevens's perception that "Death is the mother of beauty." In this context, the connotations of youth, vigor, and fecundity in Stevens's original eighth line, "Full of first longing for her," were inappropriate. Nor does "first longing" seem a very maternal emotion. Arensberg saw this difficulty clearly, and also saw that it might be overcome by the inspired use of oxymoron: his notion of a "barren" mother allows full play to both the destructive and the nurturing aspects of our natural end (i.e. death, and the idea of death).

The changes in line 10 show both men concerned with the relation between the prosaic and the poetic. Stevens's original line balanced the literary "lark" with the offhand notation, "any bird one sees." There are two problems with this, from the point of view of meaning. First of all, one "poetic" bird (the "ugly duckling," or cygnet) is surely enough for so short a poem; two simply blur the focus. So Arensberg transformed the un-American "lark" to a "thrush." Secondly, the progression in the original lines 9 and 10, from specific birds to a casual "any bird one sees," moves in the direction of generality, which is to the point, but also toward a certain commonness, which is not. The poem is about the *un*common vision which could see a swan in "any duck in any brook." So Arensberg's revision, "What of the dove,/ Or thrush, or any singing mysteries?" retains Steven's generalizing progression, but builds instead to the more elevated suggestiveness of "singing mysteries."

The manuscript of "Sonatina to Hans Christian" shows that Stevens respected Arensberg's poetic abilities enough to solicit his criticism, and to adopt a number of his suggestions for revision. But there is another aspect of Arensberg the poet which, if less well documented, had a much deeper and more far-reaching effect on Stevens's own career. We have seen that Arensberg was a great admirer of Dante: he would publish a book-length study, *The Cryptography of Dante*, in 1921; and in the years immediately preceding his move to New York he had undertaken his own translation of the *Divine*

Comedy into English terza-rima.[6] Wallace Stevens, too, had an interest in Dante which helped to shape his poetic career. It was surely Dante he had in mind when he summarized the task facing the modern poet as he saw it: "the great poems of heaven and hell have been written and the great poem of earth remains to be written" (*NA*, 142). And if the *Divine Comedy* provided an analogy for Stevens's own "supreme fiction," it may also have suggested the most characteristic form Stevens's vision would assume: the tristich, "the stanza he made a hallmark of his work," as Samuel French Morse has remarked.[7] Apparently Stevens's first attempt to write his "great poem of earth" was the experimental poem, "For an Old Woman in a Wig" (*Palm,* 12), composed in terza-rima and in three parts. This poem was inspired, I hope to show, by Arensberg's translation of Dante.

The heart of Walter Conrad Arensberg's *Idols* (1916) was its final section of two translations: "The Afternoon of a Faun" and the "Fifth Canto of the Inferno." Arensberg had spent a year translating the Mallarmé poem, and far longer on Dante.[8] He thought of both poets together, and in his view the two translations were closely related. As his explanatory "Note to 'The Afternoon of a Faun'" declares,

> The... love-story... in "L'apres-midi d'un Faune" is in reality a philosophic allegory. "L'apres-midi d'un Faune" is one of the great dream-fictions, the greatest of which is the *Divina Commedia...* [9]

A love story, a philosophic allegory, and a dream-fiction—these terms describe both Mallarmé's poem and the *Divine Comedy* in Arensberg's view. It is perhaps easier to see the application in the first instance than the second. But *The Cryptography of Dante* interprets Dante's poem as a network of Freudian sex-symbolism, in which Dante's mother (Bella) and Beatrice are twin aspects of his allegorical quest for spiritual rebirth.[10] Dante and Mallarmé's Faun are both pursuing similar spiritual visions, in this view, through a series of symbolic, dream-like sexual encounters. The Fifth Canto of the *Inferno* was the logical selection to include in *Idols*; it epitomizes Arensberg's interpretation, for it treats the sins of sexual passion, and its set-piece is the famous love story of Paolo and Francesca.

Whatever Stevens may have thought of his friend's critical method, he clearly shared Arensberg's interest in the Fifth Canto of the *Inferno*. His manuscript poem, "For an Old Woman in a Wig," was written probably in the same year (1916), and was prompted by the story of Paolo and Francesca. The germ of Stevens's poem is contained in the words with which Francesca introduces her tragic tale:

> ... There are no greater woes
> Than the remembrances of happy days
> In misery... [11]

In "For an Old Woman in a Wig," Stevens concludes similarly of his own earthly lovers, "They shall have much to suffer in remembrance, / ... elsewhere, in a deeper dreaming," and he makes this the governing idea of his poem.

Samuel French Morse is exactly right in calling "For an Old Woman in a Wig" a "microcosm and parody of *The Divine Comedy*, its three parts making a progress from Hell to an Earthly Paradise."[12] It is clearly related in theme to "Sunday Morning," as several critics have noted.[13] But in its focus on love, and in its elegiac tone, this experimental poem also anticipates "Le Monocle de Mon Oncle." The image of the title—an old woman in a wig—calls to mind the images of decayed female beauty in the stanzas Stevens rejected from "Le Monocle de Mon Oncle":

> I peopled the dark park with gowns
> In which were yellow, rancid skeletons...
> Can I take fire from such an ash?...
> A maid of forty is no feathery girl...
>
> (*OP*, 19)

Such is the mood of Stevens's "uncle" without the jaunty irony that characterizes the published stanzas. This same regret over the loss of youth and of youthful passion informs "For an Old Woman in a Wig."

In Part I, the narrator awakes at dawn in an anguished mood. The cause of his anguish is undefined, though we could infer it from the rest of the poem. But an erasure on the manuscript shows that he is tortured by memories of a love relationship, and that he originally spoke for *both* himself *and* his lover:

> Death, ... knowing,
> Grieves [both] our spirits with too poignant grieving,
>   ... keeps on showing
>
> To our still envious memory, still believing,
> The things we knew.... [14]

"Death" actually stands for the *approach* of death; it is a metaphor for aging. Just so, hell itself becomes a metaphor for the narrator's tormented state of mind.

As he lies there in this mood, the sounds of early morning suggest to his "imagination cut by sorrow" the atmosphere of the second circle of Dante's *Inferno*. The aptness of the analogy leads him to imagine that he has awakened, like Dante, mid-way in life's journey, in a dark wood. The "swarming chitter / Of crows" outside his window becomes the whirling, wailing spirits of Dante's carnal lovers. (Dante himself compares them to various birds—starlings, crows, doves.) And the distant "creaking / Of wooden wagons" becomes the otherworldly voice of Virgil, Dante's guide to the underworld:

> ... a swarming chitter
>
> Of crows that flap away beyond the creaking
> Of wooden wagons in the mountain gutters.
> ...
>
> The young dogs bark
>
> ...
> ...   It is the skeleton Virgil utters
>
> The fates of men. Dogs bay their ghosts. The traces
> Of morning grow large and all the cocks are crowing
> And [suddenly] the sun [serenely] paces
>
> The tops of hell....

The narrator's present existence is not what vexes him; that is merely "desolate." It is the *past* which has become unendurable. He is tortured by memories of an earlier happiness, now beyond his reach:

> Hell is not desolate Italy. It closes
>
> ... above a morrow
> Of common yesterdays: a wagon's rumble,
> Loud cocks and barking dogs. It does not borrow,
>
> Except from dark forgetfulness, the mumble
> Of sounds returning...

Having found that hell is a mirror of his emotional torment, the narrator wonders whether heaven can assuage his sense of loss, but finds—in Part II— that it can not:

> Is death in hell more death than death in heaven?
>
> ... There must be spirits riven
> From out contentment by too conscious yearning.
>
> ... Such spirits are the fellows,
> In heaven, of those whom hell's illusions harry.

Thus, when he proceeds to the Earthly Paradise ("all of paradise that we shall know") in Part III, Paolo and Francesca become the pattern for *all* earthly lovers whose present passion is doomed to inevitable extinction:

> They shall have much to suffer in remembrance.

> They shall have much to suffer when the beaming
> Of the clear moons, long afterward, returning,
> Shines on them, elsewhere, in a deeper dreaming.

Stevens's final point is, of course, quite different from Dante's. He recognizes the irony in Paolo and Francesca's punishment, as Santayana puts it: "Can an eternity of floating on the wind, in each other's arms, be a punishment for lovers? That is just what their passion, if left to speak for itself, would have chosen." But unlike Dante, who would say, "abandon yourself altogether to a love that is nothing but love, and you are in hell already,"[15] Stevens addresses his lovers directly as follows:

> *O pitiful lovers of earth, why are you keeping*
> *Such count of beauty in the ways you wander?*
> *Why are you so insistent on the sweeping*
>
> *Poetry of sky and sea? Are you, then, fonder*
> *Of the circumference of earth's impounding*
> *Than of some sphere on which the mind might blunder,*
>
> *If you, with irrepressible will, abounding*
> *In . . .   wish for revelation,*
> *Sought out the unknown new in your surrounding?*

The rhetorical effect of this series of questions is strong. The speaker expresses the longing for a more ideal and lasting realm; but his impassioned plea reveals an equal sympathy for "the sweeping/ Poetry of sky and sea." William Carlos Williams praised this conclusion in a letter of June 2, 1916: "I like the last part of the old-woman-in-a-wig piece because you allow yourself to become fervent for a moment."[16] It is easy to see why Williams responded to this section. Stevens's strategy is like Williams's own in, for example, his poem "Smell!" from this same period:[17] The poet asks a series of rhetorical questions which reveal a secret joy in the behavior he purports to criticise. The resulting tension between thought and feeling resolves the poem in a way which is both ambiguous and powerful.

"For an Old Woman in a Wig" is not a successful poem. The difficult form Stevens chose to work within finally proved unsuited to his material. Terza-rima is notoriously difficult in English, and the many erasures on Stevens's manuscript bear witness to the many "fillers" he had been forced to use to accommodate the rhyme scheme. But equally hobbling was his unwieldy three-part narrative framework. The opening section is too long and awkward because Stevens was trying to do two things at once: to establish the exact Dantean parallel he intended, and at the same time to develop its metaphorical significance (his real interest). As a result neither intention is clearly realized.

The reader shares the poet's relief when, in Part Two, he is able to embark on meditation unrestrained by this narrative apparatus. And the concluding apostrophe to the "lovers of earth" is "fervent," as Williams said, precisely because it has cut loose from the cumbersome structure of Dantean allusion.

Despite its ultimate failure, however, this experimental poem looks forward to the future creation of "Notes toward a Supreme Fiction" —a far more successful attempt to write a "great poem of earth," in three parts, and in tristichs. And that great poem of Stevens's maturity may, therefore, owe its form to the friendship between Wallace Stevens and Walter Conrad Arensberg—and to that time when both men were imitating Dante in their verse, during the period of their closest friendship, in New York City in 1916.

4

Eugène Emmanuel Lemercier

An unusual example of Stevens's greater "openness" during this period is the series of poems entitled "Lettres d'un Soldat." The title and epigraphs for this series were drawn from a book of the same title by a French soldier and artist named Eugène Emmanuel Lemercier.[1] The book collects Lemercier's letters to his mother, from the time of his voluntary enlistment in the Army in August of 1914 until his final "disappearance" at the front on April 6, 1915. It records one "high-souled" young man's determined struggle, under the extreme mental and physical stress of trench warfare, to reconcile his artistic temperament with his patriotic duty.

This theme must have appealed deeply to Stevens, for nowhere else in his work does he rely so heavily on a literary source as he does in "Lettres." He took from Lemercier the chronological structure of his series, and the inspiration for each individual poem. A closer look at the nature of this poetic "collaboration" may shed some light on Stevens's state of mind during this crucial stage of his development. Unless otherwise specified, the following discussion refers to the original version of "Lettres," which once numbered at least seventeen poems, for it is here that Stevens's original conception of the series is clearest. What remains of this manuscript has been published as an Appendix to A. Walton Litz's *Introspective Voyager.*[2]

The form of "Lettres" is unique in Stevens's canon. In choosing to "adapt" the book, Stevens tied himself to a chronology more rigid than any other ordering device in his *Harmonium* period, excepting perhaps the narrative mode of "The Comedian as the Letter C." Even more unusual is the structural role of individual poems in the series. Each poem in "Lettres" is not merely a variation on its particular epigraph, as most criticism of "Lettres" has seemed to assume. Rather, each poem is meant to suggest the contents of Lemercier's letters over a period of time extending both forward and backward from the date of its epigraph. Stevens intended, it seems, to compose a poetic summary of the entire book. A few examples will show how he went about this project.

Poem V in the complete series ("Here I keep thinking of the Primitives...") relates obviously to its epigraph; both speak of field mice, and of a Japanese print. But the poem's subtitle, "Comme Dieu Dispenses De Graces," and its mention of "the Primitives," refer back to a letter of three days earlier (November 4). In a similar way, in poem VIII ("There is another mother whom I love...")Stevens seems to execute a "turn" on the epigraph, in which Lemercier addresses his mother, by speaking of Nature as a Great Mother. But this "turn" is Lemercier's own, for in a letter a few days later he writes: "Do you know that those touching traditions of the Divine Mother, so happily employed in our Christian religions, are the creations of the oldest symbolism?... the type of our Madonna is the great Demeter...."[3] As both of these examples show, Stevens deliberately alluded to passages of Lemercier's book which fell within the time period described by the dates of his preceding and following epigraphs. His main object was clearly to suggest the overall development of the book, and of Lemercier's character, rather than simply to spotlight individual moments.

With this purpose in mind, the design of the series becomes clearer, and parts of it no longer seem quite so odd. Poem XII is a good example. It exists only as a fragment, included here with a translation of its epigraph:

> I forgot to tell you that a day or two ago, during the storm, I saw the cranes coming homeward towards evening. A lull in the weather allowed me to hear their cry... [4]

> In a theatre, full of tragedy,
> The stage becomes an atmosphere
> Of seeping rose—banal machine
> In an appointed repertoire...

Both Samuel French Morse and A. Walton Litz remark on the "obliquity" of this poem.[5] But read as part of the sequence, and as a partial summary of a section of Lemercier's book, rather than as a commentary on its epigraph alone, Stevens's conception becomes perfectly straightforward. The poem follows directly upon "Death of a Soldier," whose repeated phrase, "When the wind stops," becomes the "lull in the weather" which the poem describes. The poet's attention simply shifts from the actor to the setting. At the same time, Stevens is alluding to a letter of three days earlier:

> ... What I had kept about me of my own individuality was a certain visual perceptiveness that caused me to register the setting of things, a setting that dramatised itself 'artistically' as in any stage-management...[6]

Seen in this context, Stevens's poem is no longer problematical. It simply takes Lemercier's above reflection literally, reviving the dead metaphor in the common phrase, "theater of war"; the disturbingly "oblique" relation of poem to epigraph was probably unintended. It may well be this poem's triteness of conception, rather than its "obliquity," which resulted in its deletion from the series.

It seems to me that Stevens's very *lack* of obliqueness, or irony, is the defining characteristic of "Lettres." The overall relation of the series to its source is, as we have seen, uncharacteristically straightforward. The title is not at all oblique, as Stevens's titles more often are, and though individual poems sometimes bear an ironic relation to their particular epigraphs, the attitudes expressed are generally in perfect harmony with Lemercier's book. The flip tone of Poem IX, for example, ("Hi! the creator too is blind...") deliberately contrasts with its earnest epigraph, which stresses the need to "place trust in an impersonal justice." Yet the ironic contrast, the sudden shift from consolation to hopeless fatality, is quite characteristic of Lemercier's letters of 1915. This very conflict is expressed in a brief letter a few days before the date of Poem IX:

> ... My consolations fail me in these days, on account of the weather.... I close with an ardent appeal to our love, and in the certainty of a justice higher than our own.... Yet is it even sure that moral effort bears any fruit?[7]

Stevens's humorous treatment emphasizes but does not change the quality of Lemercier's emotional predicament.

"Lettres," then, follows Lemercier's book both in its precise chronology and in its spirit. The real critical question remains: *Why* did Stevens choose to undertake a poetic adaptation of this little known book? In the first place, his choice alone indicates a desire to express himself on the subject of the War. Though Stevens's letters of this period seldom betray his concern over the international situation, his very silence on the subject is striking, and lends to his few direct pronouncements the eloquence of restraint. As he wrote at the end of a letter during World War II: "I make no reference in this letter to the war. It goes without saying that our minds are full of it" (*L,* 356).[8]

Two letters of 1918 do suggest the range of feelings the war inspired in him. The sight of troops rallying in Chattanooga roused him to unabashed patriotism: "Those that are here are splendid fellows. We cannot help doing well when we really start" (*L,* 207). Stevens generally permitted himself such unguarded enthusiasm only in the realm of aesthetics. And this uncharacteristically emotional outburst is matched, in another instance during the same month, by acute embarrassment and regret because of his failure to maintain proper self-control. He felt compelled to apologize to Harriet Monroe for his insensitive "gossip of death" while visiting her in Chicago, writing:

> ... The subject absorbs me, but that is no excuse: there are too many people in the world, vitally involved, to whom it is infinitely more than a thing to think of. One forgets this. I wish with all my heart that it had never occurred, even carelessly. (*L,* 206)

These two examples show Stevens imaginatively joining in the spirit of the war effort, but at the same time feeling strongly the inadequacy of merely "thinking of" it in comparison with the sacrifice of those who are "vitally involved." Such a sense of frustration over his own role in the war effort may have found temporary appeasement in the composition of "Lettres."

What appealed to Stevens in *Lettres* was not simply its timeliness, but more immediately the character of Lemercier himself. Lemercier was French, and so an attractive alter ego for Stevens, who read *Lettres* in the original and wrote for an audience which was also fluent in that language. On the question of his French epigraphs he wrote to Harriet Monroe: "I assume that most of your readers know French sufficiently not to need a translation" (*L,* 202). But Lemercier was above all an artist, and it is in his fine sensibility and his passion for the arts, even at the front, that he most resembles Wallace Stevens.

Lemercier's metier was painting, and evidence of his painter's eye is everywhere in his letters to his mother. In almost every letter he describes the changes in the weather and landscape and the reflections these inspire in him— a mode of imaginative activity most congenial to Stevens, who had just written the "Primordia" series.[9] And the other arts were equally important to Lemercier's life in the trenches. He continually writes about music, as in this passage of a letter three days before his death:

> Think what it was for us when we were last in the front line, to have to spend whole days in the dugout.... There, in complete darkness, night was awaited for the chance to get out. But once my fellow non-commissioned officers and I began humming the nine symphonies of Beethoven. I cannot tell what thrill woke those notes within us. They seemed to kindle great lights in the cave. We forgot the Chinese torture of being unable to lie, or sit, or stand.[10]

This iteration of the consolatory powers of music surely struck a sympathetic chord in the music-lover Stevens, as would the larger theme of which this is only one instance: Lemercier's deliberate and sustained search for consolation in a hostile world—in the love of his mother, in religion, in Nature, and (most importantly for Stevens) in art. But more remarkable in the above passage is Lemercier's unstated assumption that any group of NCOs would know by heart all of Beethoven's symphonies. It seems strange from an American point of view, and would have seemed strange in 1915 as well; but the existence and value of such cultural sophistication even at the line of battle was taken for granted by the French, and by the British, too, as Paul Fussell has shown.[11] By documenting this phenomenon Lemercier doubtless made the experience of war seem more accessible to Stevens. The world of war Lemercier describes, in which finely cultivated souls are made to shine brighter and stronger through contact with the most terrible reality, is not too far removed from the world of *Harmonium,* whose two poles would later be defined by the imaginative fulfillment of "Tea at the Palaz of Hoon," and the final emptiness of "The Snow Man."

However, it was Lemercier's literary bent, more perhaps than his love of painting or music, which first suggested to Stevens the vital relation that might exist between the soldier and the poet, a theme he would return to with great effect during the early years of the Second World War. Lemercier placed a great value on writing. His letters are testaments to the lenitive power of the literary imagination. To write a letter to his mother was to *be with* her: "When I began to write on this sheet I was a little weary and troubled, but now that I am with you I become happy."[12] And to write poetry was a life-affirming act: "I have sent you a few verses. I don't know what they are worth, but they reconciled me to life."[13] He read with equal fervor, seeking consolation for his miserable condition in works of religion and philosophy ("Spinoza is a most valuable aid in the trenches"[14]), and it was this trait Stevens first emphasized in Poem I (later excised) of "Lettres": ". . . I quote the line and page,/ I quote the very phrase my masters used." As for his reading of poetry, Lemercier wrote to his mother:

> . . . I am glad to see you like Verlaine. . . . He has been my almost daily delight both here and when I was back in Paris; often the music of his Paysages Tristes comes back to me, exactly expressing the emotion of certain hours.[15]

Verlaine also "meant a good deal" to Wallace Stevens, who later recalled carrying his verses around with him, in his head, during his younger years, like Lemercier: "There were many of his lines that I delighted to repeat" (*L,* 636). The seventh poem of "Lettres," "Lunar Paraphrase," might easily be read as Stevens's own "Paysage Triste." And it can hardly be coincidence that the epigraph to this poem is the sentence which immediately precedes the passage quoted above.

These temperamental affinities between Lemercier and Stevens probably had the strongest influence on Stevens's decision to undertake a poetic adaptation of *Lettres.* Yet Stevens's point of view does differ significantly from Lemercier's at times, as is evident in Stevens's selection and emphasis, and despite the apparent faithfulness of "Lettres" to its source. The chief weakness of the series may be traced to Stevens's inability to sympathize sufficiently with his chosen subject.

Stevens acknowledged this weakness in "Lettres" when, in March of 1918, he and Harriet Monroe "went over them together and weeded out the bad ones" (*L,* 205). Their chief concern then seems simply to have been "to make a good beginning and a good end," as Stevens defined his object in revising a later series. Together they eliminated Poem I, with its conventional rhetoric, and cut at least six poems from the end of the series, reducing the total number of poems from seventeen (at least) to nine.[16] They may have agreed to omit so many poems from the end of the original series merely in order to conclude with the powerful "Death of a Soldier." But the poems which survive from this excised group suggest another reason as well.

Lemercier was a devout Christian, as Stevens was not, so that the periods of doubt and despair the French soldier experienced as he approached his final battle were overbalanced by his firm faith. His letters are moving precisely because they record his internal struggle and triumph. In a larger, historical sense they substantiate Paul Fussell's observation that "the Great War was perhaps the last to be conceived as taking place within a seamless, purposeful 'history'... in what was, compared with ours, a static world, where the values appeared stable and where the meaning of abstractions seemed permanent and reliable."[17] What survives of the poems which were to follow "Death of a Soldier," on the other hand, indicates that Stevens was either unwilling or unable to present convincingly the traditional consolations which comforted Lemercier at the end. These two poems and a fragment do not invoke "Courage... Wisdom and Love," as Lemercier does only hours before his death.[18] Nor do they make reference to the Christian perspective. Perhaps some of the lost poems did so, as "Lunar Paraphrase" invoked the crucifixion. But if this is the case, their destruction probably indicates that Stevens found them either bad poetry or unacceptable doctrine when he "weeded out the bad ones." The surviving poems emphasize, instead, the *breaking down* of the very abstract values which sustained Lemercier. It is even possible that Stevens at one point intended to make this break down the structuring theme of "Lettres." This possibility arises when we read the first and last poems together:

> No introspective chaos... I accept:
> War, too, although I do not understand.
> And, that, then, is my final aphorism.
>
> I have been pupil under bishops' rods
> And got my learning from the orthodox.
> I mark the virtue of the common-place.
>
> I take all things as stated—so and so
> Of men and earth: I quote the line and page,
> I quote the very phrase my masters used.
>
> If I should fall, as soldier, I know well
> The final pulse of blood from this good heart
> Would taste, precisely, as they said it would.

Before battle the soldier is unquestioningly idealistic, having got his experience primarily from books. He is naive enough to assert his inner strength in the form of a "final aphorism." But the poems which follow demonstrate that it is hardly final, and that mere words are insufficient to comprehend the horror of war. By the end of "Lettres," his faith in traditional wisdom has been proven empty. Trying to come to terms with the massive carnage surrounding him, he considers two standard metaphors for death, and quickly dismisses them as false:

Death was a reaper with sickle and stone,
Or swipling flail, sun-black in the sun,
A laborer.

Or death was a rider beating his horse,
Gesturing grandiose things in the air,
Seen by a muse....

Symbols of sentiment...

"So the meaning escapes," as Stevens put it in another poem of the same time, "Metaphors of a Magnifico," which also describes the failure of imaginative conceptions to withstand the pressure of reality. Bitterly, the soldier seeks a substitute for the discredited "line" and "phrase" of his former masters:

Take this new phrase,
Men of the line, take this new phrase
Of the truth of Death—

But he loses interest even in the attempt, concluding that the "truth of Death" precludes any verbal approximation:

Death, that will never be satisfied,
Digs up the earth when want returns...
You know the phrase.

Something of the bored aesthete lingers in that final line, and its inappropriateness to its context suggests what is wrong with "Lettres": The gesture is too pat, its evasion too easy to satisfy the demands of so exacting a subject. The poem, like the series as a whole, trails off into dull irresolution. Not only Lemercier's faith, but Stevens's imaginative energy seems to have faltered before the terrible reality of war.

Stevens's drastic editing of "Lettres" demonstrates his dissatisfaction with this poetic statement on the subject of war. But the subject itself continued to haunt him, and when he returned to it at the beginning of the Second World War, the experience of writing "Lettres" was clearly in his thoughts. In his prose essay of 1941, "The Noble Rider and the Sound of Words," Stevens refers to the international upheaval of the 1910s as the very fountainhead of our contemporary consciousness:

... Reality then became violent and so remains. This much ought to be said to make it a little clearer that in speaking of the pressure of reality, I am thinking of life in a state of violence, not physically violent, as yet, for us in America, but physically violent for millions of our friends and for still more millions of our enemies, and spiritually violent, it may be said, for everyone alive. (*NA*, 26-7)

As the First World War played an important part in Stevens's poetic development, so war itself became a central metaphor in his mature poetic world. He would begin to see the poet's relation to the world as a form of combat, fought in this arena of "spiritual violence." The epilogue to "Notes Toward a Supreme Fiction" begins:

> Soldier, there is a war between the mind
> And sky, between thought and day and night. It is
> For that the poet is always in the sun,
>
> Patches the moon together in his room
> To his Virgilian cadences, up down,
> Up down. It is a war that never ends....

"The idea of an endless war as an inevitable condition of modern life," Paul Fussell has written, "would seem to have become seriously available to the imagination around 1916."[19] The First World War survives in our consciousness as the "spiritual violence" in which we live our lives. It survives in Stevens's poetry in the more aggressive posture of his imagination after the major transition of his career "from a poetry of perception to a poetry of the act of the mind."[20]

From the vantage point of 1942, Stevens could see that part of the trouble with "Lettres" had been that he was trying to do two contradictory things at once:

> The immense poetry of war and the poetry of a work of the imagination are two different things. In the presence of the violent reality of war, consciousness takes the place of the imagination.... and constitutes a participation in the heroic.[21]

Stevens did not want to write war poetry, but "poetry of a work of the imagination." To do so in an atmosphere of "spiritual violence" meant that the poet must take an aggressive, combative stance toward the "pressure of reality." The new attitude he demanded of himself went against his natural inclinations. In 1918 he had apologized at length for his "gossip of death" during a time of war, because "there are many, vitally involved, for whom death is much more than something to think about." This recantation, however admirably motivated, made the common assumption that mental activity is essentially passive, and can never be considered as "vital" as the physical involvement of the soldier. The later Stevens would assert, on the contrary, that poetic activity must be "a violence from within that protects us from a violence without. It is the imagination pressing back against the pressure of reality" (*NA,* 36). The problems Stevens first confronted in "Lettres" became, in their transformation, a permanent part of his poetic landscape.

In "Lettres" Stevens first explored the close relation which existed in his mind between the soldier and the poet. The series ultimately failed because he did not get the relationship "right." He tried to identify himself with Lemercier, but was unable to present convincingly the soldier's sustaining beliefs; and the nature of this project prevented him from substituting an alternative "supreme fiction," even if the idea had occurred to him at this early stage in his career. Years later, when he returned to this theme, he would no longer try to unite the soldier and poet in a single person. In the epilogue to "Notes toward a Supreme Fiction," the two roles are separate but complementary. Soldier and poet represent the two extremes of human endeavor, on the parallel fronts of imagination and reality:

> ... The two are one.
> They are a plural, a right and left, a pair,
> Two parallels that meet if only in
>
> The meeting of their shadows, or that meet
> In a book in a barrack, a letter from Malay....

Their points of contact are spiritual ("the meeting of their shadows") and specifically literary: The soldier writes letters (like Lemercier's) which may inspire the poet, and the poet writes poems which can sustain the soldier even at the front. The complementary acts of reading and writing are made to figure the proper relation between poet and soldier, as well as between imagination and reality. And "Notes..." itself becomes the battlefield on which the impossible meeting of these "parallels" is momentarily achieved.

The epilogue to "Notes" is also, in a sense, the epilogue to "Lettres." The soldier addressed is a Frenchman ("Monsieur") like Lemercier, and he depends on language in the same vital way. The soldier in "Lettres" was prepared to sacrifice his life for the traditional values of his "masters":

> I quote the line and page,
> I quote the very phrase my master used.
>
> If I should fall, as soldier, I know well
> The final pulse of blood from this good heart
> Would taste, precisely, as they said it would.

This self-assurance ultimately failed in "Lettres." Words finally proved insufficient to sustain either the soldier or the series of poems. But the epilogue to "Notes" corrects this failure, filling the place of Lemercier's "masters" by means of the poet's "supreme fiction," and reasserting the power of language to redeem even "the final pulse of blood".[22]

> ... Monsieur and comrade,
> The soldier is poor without the poet's lines,
>
> His petty syllabi, the sounds that stick,
> Inevitably modulating, in the blood....

The transition from "Lettres" to "Notes" is simple but profound. And it is perhaps easiest to see by comparing the tone of resigned disillusionment, the uncompelling rhythms, and the vague meaning of the earlier ending:

> Death, that will never be satisfied,
> Digs up the earth when want returns...
> You know the phrase.

With the confident strength of the epilogue to "Notes":

> How simply the fictive hero becomes the real;
> How gladly with proper words the soldier dies,
> If he must, or lives on the bread of faithful speech.

5

Donald Evans

Criticism of Wallace Stevens has given only cursory attention to his friendship with Donald Evans (1884-1921), for the good reasons that this forgotten poet wrote distinctly minor verse, and that very little was known about his life or about the nature of his relationship with Stevens. New evidence suggests, however, that this friendship meant a great deal to Stevens himself. In an unpublished letter addressed to Ferdinand Reyher, on the occasion of Evans's sudden death (at the age of 39) in 1921, Stevens expressed with uncharacteristically direct emotion his distress over Evans's personal misfortune, and his respect for Evans as an artist. "He was one of the great ironists," he wrote, "one of the pure littérateurs."[1] Such tribute commemorates a friendship that was clearly important to Stevens. It therefore becomes important for us to ask what role Evans played in Stevens's life, and what influence he might have had on the development of *Harmonium*.

Although the name of Donald Evans is now virtually unknown, he had an impressive reputation in the 1910s. His poetry was admired by poets as diverse and well known as Edwin Arlington Robinson, Amy Lowell, and Ezra Pound.[2] Among Wallace Stevens's other literary friends in New York, Evans was considered a master of the lyric poem. "For us, if an American Lovelace exists, it is Donald Evans," wrote Paul Rosenfeld; Alfred Kreymborg had the highest praise for Evans's sonnets—"the form no American has ever surpassed him in"; and to Witter Bynner he seemed a true poetic pioneer: "Evans opened a new field in poetry and deserves in my judgment much more homage than he has been given."[3]

We know that Evans was important to Wallace Stevens in the 1910s because people who knew both men often thought of them together. Arthur Davison Ficke, one of Stevens's poet-friends from Harvard, recalled that Stevens was one of "the chief persons who played around with Donald Evans when I knew him." And Pitts Sanborn, who was perhaps Stevens's closest friend from this period, included both Evans and Stevens among the seven dedicatees of his book, *Vie de Bordeaux*.[4] Mutual friends also noted distinct similarities between Stevens's and Evans's poetry. Alfred Kreymborg found

Stevens's indebtedness to Evans in "Le Monocle de Mon Oncle" "unmistakable"; Witter Bynner claimed that Evans "had a decided influence on Stevens"; and William Carlos Williams went so far as to claim that Evans "was the poet to whom Stevens was for a time most indebted."[5]

Stevens's own praise of Evans as a "great ironist" and "pure littérateur" is sufficient evidence of his professional respect for this fellow poet. And the depth of this respect is suggested by the fact that Stevens once planned to collaborate with Evans on a book of poems. Stevens confided this information to Yvor Winters in a letter since destroyed, as Winters recalled years later in response to an inquiry from Stevens's daughter, Holly:

> [He] and Donald Evans had once planned to write a volume of one-line poems, but had begun almost at once to quarrel about where the poems would go on the page and so had never written the poems.[6]

This was doubtless one of the briefest collaborations in literary history, and one can sense Stevens's amusement even in Winters's telling of the anecdote. But the incident clearly shows that the two men shared (or felt they shared) sympathetic views concerning poetry. The nature of this proposed collaboration also suggests one specific area where their poetic interests coincided: they planned to collaborate on a book of *one-line* poems. Such poems would necessarily be epigrammatic—a quality both men valued.

Stevens had a "lifelong passion for aphoristic statements and gnomic utterances," as A. Walton Litz has shown. Stevens's personal library contained numerous books of "aphorisms, proverbs, or pithy journal entries"; he kept commonplace books in which he recorded quotations from his reading; and throughout his career he kept notebooks of phrases and aphorisms, of his own contriving, which would often reappear later in his poems.[7] One such list of phrases, headed "Schemata," dates from the *Harmonium* period and contains such fruitful entries as "The Idea of a Colony" (the germ of "The Comedian as the Letter C"?), "Hymn from a watermelon pavilion," and "Poetry supreme fiction." Stevens's titles are often one-line poems in themselves: "The Emperor of Ice-Cream," "Oak Leaves are Hands," "The Planet on the Table." Donald Evans shared this "lifelong passion" for aphorism. He kept a notebook of brief quotations from his reading, lists of words culled from dictionaries, and phrases of his own.[8] His sonnets are sometimes virtually centos of these phrases, and they are usually epigrammatic—their characteristic verbal units are the line or the couplet.

But Stevens's moving eulogy of Evans, quoted above, was surely inspired by something more substantial than a common love of epigram. The statement is both thoughtful and reticent, suggesting that Stevens was recording what seemed to him the essential qualities of Evans's character: "He was one of the great ironists, one of the pure littérateurs." What does this commendation mean in the context of Evans's life and art?

A "pure littérateur" is a man wholeheartedly devoted to the literary life. The phrase aptly describes what we know of Donald Evans. Our earliest record of him—a journal he kept in 1904-5, at the age of 19—reveals an uncompromising determination to become a poet, despite the disapproval of his family and the necessity of full-time employment to support himself. Once he finally published his first book of poems, in 1912, he worked assiduously and published four more books over the next six years, until personal and financial hardship overtook him. But even in letters written only days before his premature death in 1921, his chief concern was to find time, somehow, to continue writing poetry.[9]

The phrase, "pure littérateur," probably had further implications. Stevens was familiar with Evans's poetry well before he met Evans himself, as Walter Conrad Arensberg told Carl Van Vechten in 1914:

> ... Walter explained how he, Stevens, had wanted to meet me, finding something intriguing about my style, while Donald Evans he felt he fully understood from his writing and a *rencontre* would not make understanding more complete.[10]

Though Van Vechten seems not to realize it, the comparison he records is not flattering to himself as a writer. Stevens's notion that a *"rencontre"* with Evans "would not make understanding more complete" was typical of his attitude toward things which engaged his imagination deeply. In much the same way, he loved the city of Paris, and felt he knew it though he would never see it. "I suppose that if I ever go to Paris the first person I meet will be myself since I have been there in one way or another for so long...." (*L,* 665). Stevens had clearly read Evans's poetry with enough interest that the poet seemed to live fully in his imagination, and the personality expressed in Evans's poems seemed synonymous with Evans himself, the "pure littérateur."

The personality Stevens felt he "fully understood" in 1914 was the Evans of the *Sonnets from the Patagonian* and of his few *Trend* poems; it was the carefully contrived pose of a "great ironist." Evans had deliberately invented this personality for himself in 1913, and maintained it with difficulty while he remained in New York, until late 1915. Before 1913, he had been "conventionally dressed and with conventional manners," as Van Vechten recalled, but in the wake of the Armory Show and after the advent of Gertrude Stein he adopted the stylized manner of a dandy/poseur in both his poetry and his life.[11] He drank "wicked" absinthe, wore a monocle, and installed a little dressing table in his room—"very Eighteenth Century," according to Louise (Norton) Varèse.[12] Arthur Davison Ficke summarized the transformation: "His literary life was one of the most interesting series of poses."[13] Evans's object, as he described it in the Patagonian sonnet entitled, "The Immortal Pose," was to create "The perfect pose that no man dare forget,/ A teasing mask that none can tear away." The mask had a dual purpose: to make an indelible impression on the observer, and to protect or conceal the wearer. Accordingly, it both attracted and repelled. Evans's publishing partner, Otto Theis, addressed this seeming contradiction in Evans's character: "Donald was so amazingly complex a personality—in which extraordinary charm and grotesque diablerie were so confusingly mingled—that it is hard to present a real picture of his character."[14]

Evans's pose was further complicated by the double life he was compelled to lead in order to maintain it. He worked fulltime as a journalist his entire adult life (excepting his period of military service during the First World War), and pursued an active literary life during his off-hours. Because the time he could devote to writing was so limited, most of his literary friendships (even with such close friends as Witter Bynner and Arthur Davison Ficke) were conducted almost entirely through letters. In this respect his life is similar to Stevens's. And Amy Lowell can not have been the only one to consider both poets poseurs.[15] But Evans's extension of the literary pose to include his daily life was unlike Stevens, though it may have been one of the things Stevens meant in praising him as a "pure littérateur."

Evans's double life was maintained at great personal cost. He borrowed money to found his short-lived Claire Marie Press in 1913, and habitually overworked himself. He drank heavily to offset fatigue and disappointment, a habit which soon compounded his difficulties. His literary "mask" became a necessary refuge. Explaining the genesis of his "Patagonian" manner to Arthur Davison Ficke, from the vantage point of 1916, Evans recalled that during his New York years, "the fates decreed for me such a complicated existence with so much that was unbearably ugly and heartsearing that I had to turn many odd corners of irony to keep sane."[16] And years later Louise (Norton) Varèse reflected that if Evans had not "made this character up for himself" he would probably have committed suicide sooner.[17] Like Wallace Stevens's "Weeping Burgher," Evans was impelled to distort a too-harsh reality:

> It is with a strange malice
> That I distort the world....
>
> The sorry verities!
> Yet in excess, continual,
> There is cure of sorrow.

The persona of Donald Evans's *Sonnets from the Patagonian* was his most effective creation, and he became identified with it. He tried to break away from it in his later books, aiming at a more straightforward style. But the effect was bland, and people remembered him only as the author of the witty, ironic *Sonnets*. Paul Rosenfeld, when he wrote a eulogy of Evans in 1925, titled it "An American Sonneteer," apparently unaware of Evans's last two books. Evans eventually succumbed, it seems, to popular expectation. When he returned to New York after the War, he could not afford to attend many literary gatherings, because of his disastrous family life and too-demanding job. But at a party in 1921, fortunately recorded by Alfred Kreymborg, Evans was again reciting the *Sonnets*—eight years after he had written them.[18] To Wallace Stevens, who was present on that occasion, Evans seemed to have regained all his old vigor. But it was the Patagonian persona Stevens saw, for in a few weeks Evans had taken his own life.

Donald Evans's Patagonian persona derived from the English 1890s, and particularly from Oscar Wilde who was (in Richard Le Gallienne's phrase) "the incarnation of the spirit of the 90s."[19] It was Wilde's *Poems* (1881) which most impressed Evans, as this journal entry from 1904 reveals:

> Read Oscar Wilde's Dorian Gray—it pained me considerably—O had he died in 1881! For Poems are precisely immortal and—forgotten! The irony of that![20]

This passage explains the conception of a poem from Evans's first book, *Discords* (1912), entitled: "Elegiac: O___W___, Obit A.D. 1881."[21] Like the Wilde of the *Poems*, Evans's persona is a dandy and a poseur—he acts a role with as much style as he devotes to his clothes ("cloaked he comes in a new attitude," p. 49).[22] The ostensible goal of such an enterprise is to extend aesthetic criteria to one's daily life, but the underlying motive is self-defense: the poseur fears that sincerity will make him vulnerable. Accordingly, when his pose is challenged, he reacts with undiminished theatricality:

> And when discovery marred the best disguise
> He winced a sigh, bowed to spoiled deceit,
> And donned the damask draperies of defeat
> To woo dishonor as an enterprise. (p. 55)

Not surprisingly, both Wilde and Evans devote sonnets to actresses, as fellow-spirits.[23] Wilde's "Phèdre: to Sarah Bernhardt" stressed the otherworldliness of such professionals: "How vain and dull this common world must seem/ To such a One as thou. . . ." And Evans's "Theatre du Nord" depicts the concomitant hazard of a life of posing:

> She was tired to tears, and yet there were no tears,
> Only the dead seas of indifference . . .
> The woman raged to touch the flame once more,
> But the worn-out emotions could not stab. (p. 27)

Metaphorically, the emotional exhaustion of the dandy-poseur reflects the spiritual exhaustion of the age—it is the personal equivalent of the general "melancholy, long, withdrawing roar" Matthew Arnold heard in the ebbing "sea of faith."[24] Without the support of a commonly accepted mythology, the individual is left to "act" continually without deep conviction. As Wallace Stevens put it in "Meditation" (*Others,* December 1917):

> It comes to this,
> That even the moon
> Has exhausted its emotions.

In this predicament, the dandy devotes his energies to an outward show of order, offsetting metaphysical insecurity with utter confidence in his own sartorial taste. "Dandyism is the last gleam of heroism in times of decadence," claimed Baudelaire.[25] And when at length Wallace Stevens devised his own paradoxical solution to this problem—his notion of the "supreme fiction"—it was an "exquisite" formulation tailored to fit the dandy/poseur:

> The final belief is to believe in a fiction, which you know to be a fiction, there being nothing else. The exquisite truth is to know that it is a fiction and that you believe in it willingly. (*OP,* 163)

The poem of Stevens's *Harmonium* period which owes the most to Evans's "pose" in the *Sonnets from the Patagonian* is "Le Monocle de Mon Oncle." In May of 1918, while the First World War was still raging, and probably before Stevens had begun work on "Le Monocle de Mon Oncle," (*Others,* December 1918), the N.L. Brown Company of New York published a new edition of the *Sonnets from the Patagonian.* Evans made two additions to this revised volume which significantly altered its tone: a "Preface" and two new sonnets emphasized the essential seriousness of this book which, in 1914, had seemed to many readers only a slightly perverse *jeu d'esprit.* The new "Preface" begins, "With the Allied cause crumbling away it is high time we thought of aesthetics," and continues in the same vein:

> Could I enlist a Battalion of Irreproachables, whose uniforms should be walking suit, top hat and pumps, and their only weapon an ebony stick, and sail tomorrow, we should march down Unter den Linden in a month, provided wrapped in our kerchiefs we carried the Gospel of Beauty, and a nonchalance in the knot of our cravats.[26]

Evans's "Gospel of Beauty" harks back to Wilde, as does the tone of the entire preface. When Evans writes, "With all my heart I hope I shall not come back, for then impersonally I shall have fallen for a cause in which I have no faith," he is echoing Wilde's assertion that, "I think I would more readily die for what I do not believe in than for what I hold to be true."[27]

Evans's letters from the time show that he took this "Preface" seriously, and was proud of it. He had enlisted in the Army shortly after the United States entered the War, and when he wrote the "Preface" he was awaiting orders to be sent overseas.[28] His aestheticist theme may seem to us grotesquely out of place in the context of the War, but it would surely have struck a sympathetic chord in Wallace Stevens who, as we have seen, sought to establish a close relationship between the roles of poet and soldier in the modern world. Stevens would have understood the "Preface" in the sense Evans intended: as a defense of the enduring validity of the aestheticist pose.

As Robert Buttel remarks of Evans's "Preface," "In all its preposterous exaggeration [it] reveals a serious, almost desperate, sense of the need for beauty."[29] The two new sonnets Evans added to the 1918 edition emphasize, on the other hand, a complementary dissatisfaction with daily life. "Aspens at Cresheim" depicts the death of romantic love, and "Failure at Forty" describes the despair of an aging, unsuccessful writer. These two poems throw into relief the elegiac tone of the earlier sonnets, an aspect that had been generally overlooked (in 1914) because of their more obvious Nineties "wickedness" and Steinian humor. The title, "Failure at Forty," sounds a minor note throughout the *Sonnets from the Patagonian,* whose reverberations extend to the forty-year-old, dejected narrative voice of "Le Monocle de Mon Oncle."

The title, "Le Monocle de Mon Oncle," alludes to Evans's "En Monocle," and the first stanza of Stevens's series shows what his conception owes to that particular sonnet. "En Monocle" reads:

> Born with a monocle he stares at life,
> And sends his soul on pensive promenades;
> He pays a high price for discarded gods,
> And then regilds them to renew their strife.
> His calm moustache points to the ironies,
> And a fawn-colored laugh sucks in the night,
> Full of the riant mists that turn to white
> In brief lost battles with banalities.
>
> Masters are makeshifts and a path to tread
> For blue pumps that are ardent for the air;
> Features are fixtures when the face is fled,
> And we are left the husks of tarnished hair;
> But he is one who lusts uncomforted
> To kiss the naked phrase quite unaware.

Evans's monocled personality is overly literary, and has immortal longings which mock his present, dejected state; he longs "uncomforted/ To kiss the naked phrase quite unaware." So Stevens's dejected narrator in the first stanza of "Le Monocle de Mon Oncle" experiences a vision of an unattainable but desirable goddess who is literary as well as womanly: the "radiant bubble that she was" is also a "watery syllable."

> "Mother of heaven, regina of the clouds,
> O sceptre of the sun, crown of the moon,
> There is not nothing, no, no, never nothing,
> Like the clashed edges of two words that kill."
> And so I mocked her in magnificent measure.
> Or was it that I mocked myself alone?
> I wish that I might be a thinking stone.
> The sea of spuming thought foists up again
> The radiant bubble that she was. And then
> A deep up-pouring from some saltier well
> Within me, bursts its watery syllable.

Both poems employ a literary-critical vocabulary which reflects the painful self-consciousness of the Patagonian persona: Evans speaks of "ironies" and "banalities"; Stevens speaks of "the clashed edges to two words that kill," adding in an aside, "so I mocked her in magnificent measure."

The mixture of sex and literature, speaking of poetry in terms of love, love in terms of literature, is a major theme of "Le Monocle de Mon Oncle." It was probably this quality which inspired Alfred Kreymborg to remark that Stevens's "indebtedness" to "En Monocle" in this poem was "unmistakable": "the fruit of *love*... is a *book* too mad to read" (iv); "in our *amours*... their *scrivening*/Is breathless to attend" (vi); "Like a dull scholar, I behold in *love*... This trivial *trope*" (viii); "Most venerable *heart*, the lustiest *conceit*/Is not too lusty for your broadening" (ix); "if *sex* were all... the wished for *words*" (xi).

Formally, Stevens's eleven-line pentameter stanzas in "Le Monocle de Mon Oncle" are sonnet-like. The first stanza is composed of mostly end-stopped lines, with a break after line seven, approximating the octave/sestet pattern of Petrarchan form which Evans uses in the *Sonnets from the Patagonian*. The loose structure of Stevens's series as a whole is like nothing so much as a sonnet-sequence, an appropriate form for the reflections of his disconsolate lover. And this sequence of interrelated short sections became Stevens's most characteristic longer form, suggesting a further affinity with the Evans of the *Sonnets*.

The pose of the dandy-aesthete, which informs "Le Monocle de Mon Oncle," has a double aspect which is conveniently exemplified by Oscar Wilde's sonnet, "Taedium Vitae." The dandy's exacting aesthetic standards, in this poem, make his encounters with everyday life seem torturously brutal:

> To stab my youth with desperate knives, to wear
> This paltry age's gaudy livery...
> ... to go back to that hoarse cave of strife
> Where my white soul first kissed the mouth of sin.

His only alternative is to affect disdain and boredom, to retreat from life:

> ... these things are less to me
> Than the thin foam that frets upon the sea,
> Which hath no seed: better to stand aloof
> Far from these slanderous fools ... [30]

This duality also characterizes Donald Evans's *Sonnets from the Patagonian*, and is succinctly expressed in these lines from "In the Vices":

> He streaks himself with vices tenderly;
> He cradles sin, and with a figleaf fan
> Taps his green cat, watching a bored sun span
> The wasted minutes to eternity. (p.15)

The same duality is evident in Wallace Stevens's *Harmonium*, its two poles best represented, perhaps, by the boredom of "The Man Whose Pharynx Was Bad":

> The time of year has grown indifferent.
> Mildew of summer and the deepening snow
> Are both alike in the routine I know.
> I am too dumbly in my being pent.

and by the tortured feelings of "The Weeping Burgher," "weeping in a calcined heart."

"Le Monocle de Mon Oncle" is unique in *Harmonium* because it includes both of these impulses together. This inclusiveness is remarked by Helen Vendler, who calls it

> the poem in which Stevens represses nothing, neither his sadness as he does in the *Comedian* nor his irony as he does in *Sunday Morning.* ... *Le Monocle de Mon Oncle* comes nearer to encompassing ... the whole of Stevens. [31]

It is the peculiar balance of these two moods in "Le Monocle de Mon Oncle" that distinguishes Stevens's "Patagonian" persona from the otherwise similar Laforguian persona of, for instance, T.S. Eliot's "The Love Song of J. Alfred Prufrock." As A. Walton Litz has observed, "The dandy-Pierrot of 'Le Monocle' is a less anxious and less pensive version of J. Alfred Prufrock, a mock-hero who accepts the ironies of his position and makes them tolerable through the solace of language." [32]

Using Vendler's terms, we might describe the tone of "Le Monocle de Mon Oncle" as one of elegiac irony. The narrator's ironic detachment is evident in his sense of having exhausted his emotions, having outlived life:

> The measure of the intensity of love
> Is measure, also, of the verve of earth.
> For me, the firefly's quick, electric stroke
> Ticks tediously the time of one more year. (v)

and in his professed boredom: "one merely reads to pass the time" (iv). The most direct expression of the poem's elegiac impulse is Stevens's use of interjections, for example:

> Alas! Have all the barbers lived in vain
> That not one curl in nature has survived? (iii)

The interjection of grief—"Alas!"—is qualified by its ironic context. The degree of emotion it expresses outweighs its object (the curls), thereby recalling the mock-heroism of Pope's "The Rape of the Lock" as well as Beardsley's "Barber of Meridian Street." A similar effect is achieved by the interjection, "Anguishing hour!," of stanza eleven—the narrator's comically exaggerated response to the news that sex is not "all."

In a less ironic context—a stanza from "The Naked Eye of the Aunt," probably intended to accompany "Le Monocle de Mon Oncle"—Stevens employs the Greek form of "Alas!":

> Eheu! Eheu! with what a weedy face
> Black fact emerges from her swishing dreams.

The exotic interjection may seem excessive, like much of the rhetoric in these rejected stanzas. But it reminds us, too, that the epigraph to Oscar Wilde's *Poems* was a sonnet entitled "Hélas!"—French for "Alas!" Wilde himself considered this his "most characteristic poem," according to Yeats.[33] "To call a poem'Hélas!'," observes Richard Ellmann, "to sigh in a foreign language, alerts us that the confession to follow will luxuriate in its penitence."[34] Such luxuriance is always qualified, in "Le Monocle de Mon Oncle," by careful irony, and this doubtless explains Stevens's rejection of "The Naked Eye of the Aunt."

Stevens's repeated use of interjections of grief also explains the oblique conclusion of stanza six: "It is a theme for Hyacinth alone." Hyacinth's theme is, of course, the interjection "ai-ai," written on the petals of the flower whose eponym died tragically and prematurely. Stevens uses this interjection explicitly in "Esthétique du Mal" (*CP*, 317): " ... we forego/Lament, willingly forfeit the ai-ai." Hyacinth was, according to Ovid, a youth beloved of Apollo who was transformed into this perennial symbol of lost youth and beauty. The direct literary allusion is relatively unusual in Wallace Stevens, but it is appropriate to his bookish narrator in this poem.

Lament tempered by comic irony; irony suddenly braced by genuine pathos—this is what we mean by the phrase, "elegiac irony." It describes the tone of "Le Monocle de Mon Oncle," and to some degree the very spirit of *Harmonium* itself. It was a spirit Stevens surely associated with that strange little book, *Sonnets from the Patagonian*, and with the brief life of its author, Donald Evans.

6

William Carlos Williams

The lifelong friendship between Wallace Stevens and William Carlos Williams began, most probably, in New York City in the year 1915, when both men became associated with the group responsible for the literary magazines *Rogue* and *Others*. There is no record of their first meeting, but by the time Stevens left New York for Hartford, in May of 1916, they were clearly well acquainted. No longer able to depend on meeting each other casually among "the crowd" in New York, the two men began to exchange letters. The earliest of these which survive—dated the first week of June, 1916—have the tone of a continuing conversation. "I shall take it upon myself to inform you of anything of importance doing among the crowd when we get together again," wrote Williams on June 8.

A postscript to this same letter suggests something of the nature of their relationship at this early stage. After offering some rather forceful criticisms of Stevens's poem, "The Worms at Heaven's Gate" (*CP*, 49), Williams concludes in a spirited tone: "For Christ's sake yield to me and become great and famous." The humorous exaggeration of this command is in part self-effacing. He had made substantial corrections in "The Worms at Heaven's Gate" and his boldness in doing so might be construed as youthful arrogance by the sensitive older poet. Williams knew this, and made a joke of it. But his hyperbolic insistence has a serious aspect, too, clearly indicating that he did not foresee an easy acquiescence on Stevens's part. The two poets' differing views on the subject of poetry were already, in 1916, a familiar point of contention between them. Williams could joke about this because he was sure of Stevens's friendship; he offered straightforward criticisms trusting that Stevens would accept them in the right spirit. Stevens did, in fact, "yield" to Williams in this particular instance, thereby making good the joke, and confirming the friendship.

This early interaction, occurring at a time when each poet was consciously searching for his own distinctive voice, contains the elements of a dialogue that would continue throughout their careers. Stevens's original manuscript version of "The Worms at Heaven's Gate" began:

> Out of the tomb, we bring Badroulbadour,
> Within our bellies, as a chariot...

and ended with this couplet:

> O, stallions, like a pitiless charioteer..
> *She will forget us in the crystalline.*[1]

In revising this poem the first thing Williams did was to drop the final couplet. He explained:

> I have left off the last two lines for the obvious reason that they are fully implied in the poem: the lowness of the worms, the highness of Badroulbadour. This is a weakening of the truth of the poem by a sentimental catch at the end.[2]

The criticism is just, but Williams discreetly understates the extent to which his editing has altered the meaning of the poem. The original version, like so many of Stevens's experimental poems of this period, aims at a very complex irony but falls short of its goal. The chariot, which became after Williams's editing an effective but subsidiary metaphor, was originally the central image of the poem. Having in mind, it seems, the myth of the charioteer in Plato's *Phaedrus,* which would later inspire his prose essay, "The Noble Rider and the Sound of Words," Stevens was attempting to write a modern myth of the relation between body and spirit. In that essay of 1942, Stevens would describe the modern response to Plato's myth as follows:

> The truth is that we have scarcely read the passage before we have identified ourselves with the charioteer, have, in fact, taken his place and, driving his winged horses, are traversing the whole heaven. Then suddenly we remember, it may be, that the soul no longer exists and we droop in our flight and at last settle on the solid ground. The figure becomes antiquated and rustic. (*NA,* 3-4)

Stevens's explanation for this failure of belief is that "The imagination loses vitality as it ceases to adhere to what is real. ... the imagination lost its power to sustain us. It has the strength of reality or none at all (*NA,* 6-7).

In "The Worms at Heaven's Gate" Stevens had tried to make a similar point about Plato's myth, but in a more oblique, self-consciously "poetic" manner. He depicted the imagination "los[ing] vitality as it ceases to adhere to what is real," from the point of view of "reality" itself (the worms, or death) which is thereby forgotten. Badroulbadour is the "pitiless charioteer," and the speaker of the poem is one of the worms who are at once her "chariot" and her "stallions." As in "Disillusionment of Ten O'Clock," where Stevens depicted the atrophied modern imagination in the form of a comic lament by a too-fastidious connoisseur of eccentricity, so in "The Worms at Heaven's Gate" he tried to make a dandyish pose express a simple, paradoxical truth. Here the disvaluation of the natural world in the Christian scheme of things ("Heaven") is presented as the sentimental lament of the natural forces (the worms) at their own rejection:

> O, stallions, like a pitiless charioteer . .
> *She will forget us in the crystalline.*

Unlike "Disillusionment of Ten O'Clock" however, Stevens's conception here suffuses not the entire poem, but only the final lines.

In citing his reasons for excising these lines, Williams appealed to the orthodox modernist distrust of sentimentality and unmasculine weakness, rightly assuming that Stevens would assent to this rationale. But Williams's quarrel with the poem may well have had deeper roots. He probably would not have objected to Stevens's ironic use of classical myth to express a modern viewpoint, for his own "Postlude" had done exactly that, and had won Ezra Pound's unstinting praise. But the dandy-like posturing of the speaker in the final lines surely seemed to Williams an unwelcome relic of the Nineties. The self-pitying tone of the final couplet discolors the rest of the poem causing the catalogue of Badroulbadour's bodily attributes to read like the lisping fussiness of an overrefined aesthete. There is a grotesque irony in the application of such a niggling tone to a dead body, and in making it issue from the mouth of a worm, which brings to mind the failed manuscript poems "Headache" and "Dolls." Williams was quick to locate the source of the problem in the final couplet, and to see that the real strength of the poem lay elsewhere than in its self-conscious strangeness.

Typically, Williams's corrections demonstrate the Imagist principles of clarity and concentration. The success of his efforts in this instance is perhaps best measured by the only other change he made in the poem. He wrote:

> I have changed line two from:
> > "Within our bellies, as a chariot,"
> to the following:
> > "Within our bellies, we her chariot,"
>
> I think the second version is much the better for the reasons that THE WORMS ARE HER CHARIOT and not only seem her chariot. Then again: "bellies" "as a chariot" (plural and singular) sounds badly while "we her chariot" has more of a collective sense and feels more solid. What do you say?[3]

The weak and impersonal simile, "as her chariot," becomes the more tightly worked metaphor, "*we her* chariot," the personal pronouns implying in a single phrase what was so obviously stated in the original ending: "*She* will forget *us* in the crystalline." At the same time, the greater force of the new phrasing recaptures for Stevens's chariot-image some of the importance he had intended it to have in the poem, thereby reducing the possibility of his annoyance at the deletion of the final couplet. Williams's seemingly minor change is a textbook demonstration of the Imagist doctrine that verbal concision is a source of poetic strength.

In editing "Worms," Williams made it, in effect, more like one of his own poems. His chief concern was to achieve greater strength of phrasing, and in order to do so he reduced Stevens's overly intricate conception to a simpler design. The revised poem is less complex in thought, more intense in its immediate impact. It is interesting to compare Williams's editorial efforts, in this respect, with Ezra Pound's editing of Eliot's "The Waste Land." Donald Gallup summarizes that more famous collaboration:

> ... The poem which resulted from the Eliot-Pound collaboration was in some respects quite different from that which Eliot had had in mind. At least part of what the central poem gained in concentration, intensity, and general effectiveness through Pound's editing was at the sacrifice of some of its experimental character.[4]

According to Eliot, the "collaborative" impulse which we have noted in the early Wallace Stevens, was general among the avant-garde poets of the 1910s, and was the direct result of Pound's influence:

> Pound... created a situation in which, for the first time... English and American poets collaborated, knew each other's works, and influenced each other.... If it had not been for the work that Pound did in the years (1910-1922)... the isolation of American poetry, and the isolation of individual American poets, might have continued for a long time.[5]

The collaboration of Stevens and Williams on "The Worms at Heavens' Gate" supports this view. Williams's editing exhibits both the spirit and the particular stylistic precepts of his friend Ezra Pound.

This early episode already reveals one aspect of the poetic differences which were the basis of a respectful but lifelong literary quarrel between Stevens and Williams. From the vantage point of 1953, Stevens could express the source of their disagreement quite simply: "Bill Williams... rejects the idea that meaning has the slightest value and describes a poem as a structure of blocks" (*L,* 803). The first half of the criticism is phrased more judiciously in an earlier letter: "I have the greatest respect for [Williams], although there is the constant difficulty that he is more interested in the way of saying things than in what he has to say" (*L,* 544). Hugh Kenner has called this "one of the most extraordinary misunderstandings in literary history."[6] But if so, it is a misunderstanding which Williams himself sometimes shared. Summing up his career in 1954, in the Preface to his *Selected Essays,* he would write: "It is not what you say that matters, but the manner in which you say it; there lies the secret of the ages."[7] He might have written this epigram in 1916 as justification for his editing of "The Worms at Heaven's Gate."

A corollary to Stevens's charge that Williams undervalues "meaning" is that he places too much value on form: "[he] describes a poem as a structure of blocks." Throughout his career Williams was an outspoken champion of poetic "causes" which were primarily concerned with form: Imagism, free verse, objectivism, the "variable foot." Stevens, on the other hand, had little to say about form, declaring himself "indifferent" to it: " . . . I have never felt that form matters enough to be controlled by it" (*L,* 817). Despite these differences, however, the two poets never seem to have had much difficulty reaching an agreement over whether a particular poem—the concrete instance before them—was either good or bad poetry. Their disagreement usually focused on the more abstract question of how to go about writing poems.

This is true of their famous argument in the "Prologue" to Williams's *Kora in Hell: Improvisations,* where Williams has the first word:

> The true value is that peculiarity which gives an object a character by itself. The associational or sentimental value is the false. Its imposition is due to lack of imagination, to an easy lateral sliding. The attention has been held too rigid on the one plane instead of following a more flexible, jagged resort. It is to loosen the attention, my attention since I occupy part of the field, that I write these improvisations. Here I clash with Wallace Stevens.[8]

Stevens would certainly have agreed that the "true value is that peculiarity which gives an object a character by itself." He seems, in fact, to have had this passage in mind when he wrote years later, " . . . a poem must have a peculiarity, as if it was the momentarily complete idiom of that which prompts it, even if that which prompts it is the vaguest emotion." But Williams's plan to "loosen the attention" was not, he felt, the way to achieve this end, for he continued: "This character seems to be one of the consequences of concentration" (*L,* 500). It is precisely this notion Williams objected to as "too rigid" in Stevens's letter of April 9, 1918, excerpted in the "Preface":

> . . . My idea is that in order to carry a thing to the extreme necessary to convey it one has to stick to it; . . . Given a fixed point of view, realistic, imagistic or what you will, everything adjusts itself to that point of view; and the process of adjustment is a world in flux, as it should be for a poet. But to fidget with points of view leads always to new beginnings and incessant new beginnings lead to sterility.[9]

In a postscript Stevens described this letter as "quarrelsomely full of my own ideas of discipline." And it was Stevens's exacting sense of discipline which Williams thought hobbled his imagination. His criticism of Stevens over the years continually harks back to this point: "The whole book shows the too rigid selection which Stevens feels is his virtue" (1937); "May his will decay as he ages and his daemon get more and more the upper hand" (1940); "From the first his poems invoke only one mood, restraint" (1956).[10] This fundamental disagreement helps to define the differing outlines of their poetic careers. Stevens's "fixed point of view" would eventually become his over-arching concept of the "supreme fiction" which, though its individual poetic manifestations "must change," nevertheless remains the fundamental ordering principle of his poetry as a whole. Williams's desire to "loosen the attention" reflects, on the other hand, his contrary determination to immerse his poetic self in the "world of flux," a plan he announced in "The Wanderer" (1914) and followed consistently thereafter. The irreconcilable positions they debated in the "Prologue" to *Kora in Hell* became, over the years, the defining characteristics of their separate careers.

This basic difference in poetic outlook is evident, of course, in their poetry of the 1910s. A good example is Stevens's "Six Significant Landscapes," because it was among the poems which Williams selected for *Others* of March 1916, and because it is the only other of Stevens's poems we know Williams revised. It was originally titled "Eight Significant Landscapes," but Williams cut two sections which read:

V

Wrestle with morning-glories
O, muscles!
It is useless to contend
With falling mountains.

VI

Crenellations of mountains
Cut like strummed zithers;
Dead trees do not resemble
Beaten drums.

Robert Buttel is generous in characterizing these lines as "merely ingenious."[11] Their omission is of little critical interest, as Williams acknowledged when returning the manuscript to Stevens on June 2, 1916, with the perfunctory comment, "Its alright [sic] to wrestle with morning glories but all mountains are not falling etc. (the usual bunk.)"[12] But in a letter to Harriet Monroe, in May of the same year, Stevens used two of these lines to illustrate the theme of his play, "Three Travelers Watch a Sunrise":

... The play is simply intended to demonstrate that just as objects in nature offset us, as, for example,

Dead trees do not resemble
Beaten drums,

so, on the other hand, we affect objects in nature, by projecting our moods, emotions, etc. . . .
(*L,* 195)

"The lines remind us," observes A. Walton Litz, "that Stevens' plays were concerned with the same theme of man's relationship to his physical and intellectual climate that he was exploring in his poetry."[13] This theme was central not only to Stevens's writing during his *Harmonium* period, but also to that of Williams during the same years (1914-23). It will provide a convenient focus for a comparison of the two poets, beginning with a section from "Six Significant Landscapes":

IV

When my dream was near the moon,
The white folds of its gown
Filled with yellow light.
The soles of its feet
Grew red.
Its hair filled
With certain blue crystallizations
From stars,
Not far off.

Poem IV describes the effect of a moonlit night on the mind of the poet. His environment colors the poet's image of himself, at once defining his mood and expanding his sense of order so that the very stars seem "Not far off." The influence of the "physical and intellectual climate" on the poet is figured in articles of dress, as it is in Poem VI of this series, in "Disillusionment of Ten O'Clock," and in "I have lived so long with the rhetoricians." Similarly, in Williams's "Summer Song" (*Poetry,* November 1916), the poet contemplates the moon in a morning sky, associating it with himself (the "Wanderer"), and imagining the effect of "putting on" its colors:

Wanderer moon
Smiling
A faintly ironical smile
At this brilliant,
Dew-moistened
Summer morning—
A detached,
Sleepily indifferent
Smile,
A wanderer's smile—
If I should
Buy a shirt
Your color, and
Put on a necktie
Sky-blue,

> Where would they carry me?
> Over the hills and
> Far away?
> Where would they carry me?

The similar theme of these two poems throws into relief their differences. In both poems the moon retains some of its traditional association with the imagination. It inspires in Stevens an imaginative flight heavenward with deliberately eccentric details; in Williams, a colloquial address to the moon as a fellow-wanderer over the earth. These responses are in some ways typical. Stevens's interest in the theme of man's relation to his environment—in *Three Travelers Watch a Sunrise, Carlos Among the Candles,* the "Primordia" series, etc.—was primarily theoretical and speculative, prefiguring his later philosophical considerations of the relation between reality and the imagination. Williams, on the other hand, came early to the conclusion that poetry must depict "the individual in his primary relation to place,"[14] and determined to involve himself personally with his local environment, both in his life and in his art.

Williams's moon is in a morning sky. It is an appropriate emblem of the imagination, having outlasted the darkness (its traditional context, the old order), finding its proper role in a strange context, the new day of the modern world. He liked this image, and made use of a similar one in another poem of the same time, "El Hombre" (*Others,* December 1916):

> It's a strange courage
> you give me, ancient star—
> shining alone in the sunrise
> toward which you lend
> no part.

Sometime during the next year Williams revised this poem for inclusion in *Al Que Quierel,* improving it with his customary attention to form and strength of phrase:

> It's a strange courage
> you give me, ancient star:
>
> Shine alone in the sunrise
> toward which you lend no part!

Stevens was impressed with the new version, as Williams remembered:

Wallace Stevens wrote a letter praising it and used it as a first verse in one of his own poems. I was deeply touched.[15]

The poem Williams refers to, "Nuances of a Theme by Williams" (*CP,* 18), appeared in the *Little Review,* December, 1918. Williams apparently did not see this tribute until it was published. He acknowledged it in a letter to Stevens dated Christmas Eve, 1918: "Thanks for your 'criticism' in *L. R.*" As Williams recognized, "Nuances" is an exercise in constructive criticism much like his own "editing" of "The Worms at Heaven's Gate." The chief difference between these two instances is that Stevens's "corrections" in "Nuances" are characteristically concerned more with the poem's meaning than with its form.

Stevens omitted the title of "El Hombre" in order to focus more clearly on the principle subject of the poem, the image of the star, and to draw out more precisely the "nuances" of its meaning. That meaning, as both Williams and Stevens would surely have agreed, is that the "uniqueness" of the star is its "true value"—"that peculiarity which gives an object a character by itself," as Williams put it in the "Prologue" to *Kora in Hell.* By using as his title the Spanish phrase for "The Man," Williams seems to have intended the further point (made also in the "Prologue") that the poet (the speaker) is also only "part of the field," and from that perspective embodies the same "uniqueness" as the object he perceives. Stevens dropped the title because it might also suggest a too-easy identification of the star with the speaker, thereby confusing the distinction between them which is the primary point of the poem.

The two stanzas Stevens appended to "El Hombre" are directed toward the same end. They dismiss the possible suggestion of a romantic sympathy between star and man by drawing out the colder, more modern "nuances" of Williams's poem. The first stanza corrects the false implication that the star might "mirror" the speaker, i.e. take on human qualities through sentimental projection:

> Shine alone, shine nakedly, shine like bronze,
> that reflects neither my face nor any inner part
> of my being, shine like fire, that mirrors nothing.

The second stanza counters the reverse implication, that the star might "lend' its own qualities to the speaker:

> Lend no part to any humanity that suffuses
> you in its own light.
> Be not chimera of morning,
> Half-man, half-star.
> Be not an intelligence,
> Like a widow's bird
> Or an old horse.

In each case, the purpose is to isolate the bare reality of the star, the "peculiarity which gives an object a character by itself."

This open criticism in the pages of the *Little Review* is one example of the poetic dialogue between Williams and Stevens which would continue, in less obvious manifestations, throughout their lives. Williams's "This Florida: 1924," for instance, addressed to "Hibiscus," seems clearly to be a response to Stevens's "Hibiscus on the Sleeping Shores"; and Stevens's "Spaniard of the rose" in the fourth section of "Esthétique du mal" may well be William Carlos William in disguise.[16] An episode from this dialogue toward the end of Stevens's *Harmonium* period discovers the two poets at their eternal debate over the uses of the imagination and the proper province of poetry. Some background is necessary to set the scene for this exchange.

The first issue of Williams's magazine *Contact* (edited with Robert McAlmon) appeared in December of 1920. The title was intended to refer to

> the essential contact between words and the locality that breeds them.... We seek only contact with the local conditions which confront us. We believe that in the perfection of that contact is the beginning not only of the concept of art among us but the key to the technique also.[17]

Wallace Stevens naturally admired their intention to treat the problem of man's relation to his immediate environment as the writer's central concern; the same problem had engaged him for years. But he distrusted the provincial implications of what he saw as their exclusively American bias. It seemed to him that *Contact* began well but never progressed beyond a narrow kind of aesthetic patriotism.[18] This criticism is much the same as that he later directed at Imagism: "If you are an imagist, you make a choice of subjects that is obviously limited" (*OP*, 220). Nor did he share Williams's unqualified faith in the value of "contact," as he understood it. Writing to Harriet Monroe on January 30, he referred to the second issue of *Contact:*

> This has not been a good year for poetry with me for I have never before been so busy. Whatever Dr. Williams may say about being... adrift, finding a place in abstraction sensually realized through
> CONTACT
> —there can be a little too much of it.[19]

The doctor from Rutherford could write daily even in the midst of his demanding work schedule. "Williams, I believe, writes every day or night or both, and his house must be full of manuscript, but it is quite different with me," wrote Stevens (*L,* 271). Stevens needed leisure and quiet in order to produce poetry. This reflects a basic difference of temperament which is evident, too, in their ideas of what poetry should be.

On January 24, 1922, Stevens sent a poem called "Stars at Tallapoosa" (*CP,* 71) to Alfred Kreymborg, who was then editing *Broom* in Italy.[20] Like the other poems we have considered in this chapter, it deals with the relation of the mind to the external world, and draws its imagery from the heavens:

> The lines are straight and swift between the stars....
>
> The mind herein attains simplicity.
> There is no moon, on single, silvered leaf.
> The body is no body to be seen
> But is an eye that studies its black lid....

It is not the stars themselves, but the abstract "lines" he imagines between them, which hold Stevens's attention. The poet has glimpsed a congruity between his inner and outer worlds, and his imagination responds with a sudden, abstract vision of order. The stars are merely the occasion for this interior epiphany. The artist's imagination transforms them, as it does the "glassy lights" in Stevens's later poem, "The Idea of Order at Key West," so that they seem to be "Fixing emblazoned zones and fiery poles,/ Arranging, deepening, enchanting night."

The central stanza of "Stars at Tallapoosa" contrasts the abstract beauty of these imaginary "lines"—straight, swift, sharp—with the haphazard outlines of nature. And the final stanzas refine the metaphor, expressly stating that nothing in nature (not even the stars themselves) can offer such fulfillment as that of the unfettered imagination:

> The melon-flower nor dew nor web of either
> Is like to these. But in yourself is like:
> A sheaf of brilliant arrows flying straight,
> Flying and falling straightway for their pleasure,
>
> Their pleasure that is all bright-edged and cold;
> Or, if not arrows, then the nimblest motions,
> Making recoveries of young nakedness
> And the lost vehemence the midnights hold.

These final stanzas were certain to antagonize Williams, who was committed to the position that the imagination can only fulfill itself effectively when it is immersed in the world of everyday reality: "abstraction" must be "sensually realized through contact." "Stars at Tallapoosa" was published in the June, 1922, issue of *Broom.* At the time Williams would have read this issue, he was at work on the poems of *Spring and All,* and one of them, "Eyeglasses" (apparently written in early July, judging from the date, "July 1, 1922," which Williams includes towards the end of the poem) seems clearly a response to Stevens's poem. The starting point of "Eyeglasses" is an epiphanic glimpse of the "universality of things"—a broadening vision like Stevens's "lines... between the stars." But in this heightened mood Williams does not direct his attention inward like Stevens; instead, his imagination is drawn outward toward the natural world around him:

> The universality of things
> draws me toward the candy
> with melon flowers that open
>
> about the edge of refuse
> proclaiming without accent
> the quality of the farmer's
>
> shoulders and his daughter's
> accidental skin, so sweet
> with clover and the small
>
> yellow cinquefoil in the
> parched places....

These lines deliberately obscure the distinctions Stevens had been so careful to define in "Stars at Tallapoosa." In Williams's view, there is no clear difference between an abstract vision and everyday reality; in fact, there is an irresistible attraction between them ("The universality of things/ *draws me toward* the candy"). Nor is there any hierarchy of "poetic" things—*any thing* is a potential subject for poetry, as he says explicitly later on in the poem: "*All this* is for eyeglasses/ to discover." So Williams's "melon flowers" blossom in "refuse," not because the one element complements the other but because they are both equally poetic. These "melon flowers" are a direct allusion to "Stars at Tallapoosa." Williams is refuting Stevens's claim that "The melon-flower nor dew nor web of either/ Is like to" the "lines" of abstract beauty in his mind. They are like, argues Williams, if you see correctly:

> It is
> this that engages the favorable
>
> distortion of eyeglasses
> that see everything and remain
> related to mathematics—

Stevens had depicted the operation of the imagination as "a kind of inspired mathematics," in Ezra Pound's phrase, straightening the crooked lines of this world behind shut eyes.[21] Williams recommends the opposite, open-eyed approach. For him the imagination thrusts outward. It is like a pair of "eyeglasses." It mediates between man and his environment, standing "between man and nature as saints once stood between man and the sky,"[22] and yet remaining "related to mathematics." And unlike the world of "Stars at

Tallapoosa," in which, as Joseph Riddel remarks, "there is no distortion in that mindless firmament beyond the human," and where the only alternative is the natural world where lines are never "straight," Williams's admits the concept of a "favorable/ distortion," that freshening which occurs when "familiar, simple things" are detached "from ordinary experience to the imagination."[23]

Williams makes a similar point in "The Rose," another poem from *Spring and All,* but in this case beginning with the particular and moving to the universal, as Joseph Riddel notes: "[He] begins with the rose . . . [and] discovers in the minutiae of its parts the flower's true universality."[24]

> The rose is obsolete
> but each petal ends in
> an edge, . . .
>
> But if it ends
> the start is begun
> so that to engage roses
> becomes a geometry—

He begins with a bow to Stevens: the rose may indeed be "obsolete" as a traditional poetic symbol, whether it signifies love, poetry itself, or simply part of the natural world which we can no longer believe is divinely ordered. But by a clever turn, he shows that what Stevens has discarded as a relic of the conventional imagination can be "related to mathematics" as well as Stevens's abstract "lines . . . between the stars": "so that to engage roses/ becomes a geometry—." And Williams does not stop there. He takes the "familiar, simple" rose and detaches it "from reality to the imagination," creating his own "imaginative reality" in which the earthly world *does* contain "lines" which correspond to the abstract beauty of Stevens's "lines . . . straight and swift between the stars":

> From the petal's edge a line starts
> that being of steel
> infinitely fine, infinitely
> rigid penetrates
> the Milky Way
> without contact—lifting
> from it—neither hanging
> nor pushing—
>
> The fragility of the flower
> unbruised
> penetrates space.

Williams's open-eyed observation of the everyday world achieves, in his own view, the same universal quality that Stevens finds only in the solitary realm of his own mind. Stevens, of course, would not agree. This episode merely extends their fundamental disagreement over Stevens's subjective "fixed point of view" and Williams's objective "field theory" which had occupied them in the "Prologue" to *Kora in Hell*.

One further development of their poetic differences occurred in 1934 when Stevens wrote the Preface to Williams's *Collected Poems: 1921-1931*. The Preface is a scrupulous eulogy. Stevens focuses his praise on three aspects of Williams's work—the romantic, the sentimental, and the "anti-poetic"— carefully qualifying each of these terms to remove any pejorative implications. Williams is "a romantic poet," yet he is "rarely romantic in the accepted sense"; and, in any case, "All poets are, to some extent, romantic poets." He has "a sentimental side" yet "What Williams gives, on the whole, is not sentiment but the reaction from sentiment, or, rather, a little sentiment, very little, together with acute reaction." And he has "a passion for the anti-poetic," but not as an "affectation" or in its "merely rhetorical aspect"; it is the natural complement of his sentimentality: "the essential poetry is the result of the conjunction of the unreal and the real, the sentimental and the anti-poetic, the constant interaction of opposites. This seems to define Williams and his poetry" (*OP*, 254-57).

The very care with which Stevens defines his terms bespeaks his great respect for Williams. But oddly, Williams took offense at this Preface, even as he recalled it in 1957:

> ... I was pleased when Wallace Stevens agreed to write the Preface but nettled when I read the part where he said I was interested in the anti-poetic. I had never thought consciously of such a thing. As a poet I was using a means of getting an effect. It's all one to me—the anti-poetic is not something to enhance the poetic—it's all one piece. I didn't agree with Stevens that it was a conscious means I was using. I have never been satisfied that the anti-poetic had any validity or even existed.[25]

"Something about the very phrase anti-poetic apparently enraged him as a poet," remarked his editor, Edith Heal.[26] He seems to have understood Stevens's use of this term as a challenge to his own position (in *Spring and All*, for instance) that *anything* is potentially poetic. In Williams's view, there can be no distinction between poetic and anti-poetic: "it's all one piece ... I have never been satisfied that the anti-poetic ... even existed."

Stevens, for his part, was probably very surprised by Williams's reaction. He had chosen the leading critical terms of his essay from Williams's own vocabulary, recalling with gratitude Williams's editing of "The Worms at Heaven's Gate." In that early collaboration, Williams's criticism was "anti-poetic" in the positive sense Stevens intends: it was aimed at curbing Stevens's romanticism and sentimentality. Explaining his excision of the final couplet, Williams had written: "This is a weakening of the truth of the poem by a sentimental catch at the end." Stevens had taken the lesson to heart, and it came to define, for him, Williams's character as a poet. As he wrote in the Preface: "To a man with a sentimental side the antipoetic is that truth, that reality to which all of us are forever fleeing" (*OP,* 255). Stevens lists this "special use of the anti-poetic" among Williams's "veritable additions to the corpus of poetry." By using the term "anti-poetic" in this sense, contrasting it not with the poetic but with the sentimental, Stevens is also deliberately recalling the opening of *Spring and All:*

> What do they mean when they say: "I do not like your poems ... There is nothing appealing in what you say but on the contrary the poems are positively repellent. ... Is this what you call poetry? It is the very antithesis of poetry. It is *antipoetry* [my italics]. It is the annihilation of life upon which you are bent. Poetry that used to go hand in hand with life, poetry that interpreted our deepest prompting, poetry that inspired, that led us forward to new discoveries, new depths of tolerance, new heights of exaltation. You moderns! it is the death of poetry that you are accomplishing ... ?"[27]

Here Williams uses the term "antipoetry" to signify the opposite of the conventional, the merely harmonious, the sentimental. And in this sense, he admits, his own work might very well be called "antipoetry": "Very well. I am not in search of 'the beautiful illusion'."[28]

Why then, did Williams react so strongly against Stevens's use of the term "anti-poetic" in 1934? It seems likely that he was angered more by the circumstances attending the publication of Stevens's essay than by what the essay said. First of all, though he had used the term "antipoetry" in a parody of certain nameless, negligible critics, its import must have seemed far more serious when applied to his work by a respected fellow poet, in the Preface to his *Collected Poems.* Secondly, the very sort of reviewers Williams had been mocking in *Spring and All* now adopted the language of Stevens's Preface and used it indiscriminately, for years afterwards, to describe Williams's method.[29] The Preface thus became a source of irritation to Williams, and in trying to place the blame he misread Stevens's essay, ironically interpreting the term "anti-poetic" in the same way as his least sympathetic reviewers.

It is a testament to the fundamental sympathy between Stevens and Williams that this misunderstanding did not cause any serious break between them. It is one part of that continuing poetic dialogue, grounded in personal friendship and professional respect, which began in New York in 1915, and would continue to stimulate and refresh both poets throughout their careers.

Conclusion

There are many aspects of Wallace Stevens which the preceding chapters have hardly touched upon. Even within the limited time period they represent there remains ample room for further exploration along the same lines. Continuing research might, for instance, reveal other, equally important "collaborators." (The most likely candidates seem to be Ferdinand Reyher and Pitts Sanborn.) A longer study might also consider Stevens's brief career as a playwright in 1916-17, and his consequent involvement with editors, directors, designers, and actors, as an example of his greater openness to influence during the 1910s. Or it might explore the relation between Stevens's poetry of 1921-22, including "The Comedian as the Letter C," and the nearly universal call for a specifically American modernism that followed the War. These and other aspects are beyond the scope of the present study. The foregoing chapters will have served their purpose if they suggest the value of seeing Wallace Stevens not as an isolated figure, but as a representative modern poet, deeply and imaginatively involved with his own time and place.

Notes

Chapter 1

1. Most of Stevens's "experimental" manuscript poems are reprinted in Robert Buttel, *Wallace Stevens: The Making of Harmonium* (Princeton: Princeton Univ. Press, 1967), and in A. Walton Litz, *Introspective Voyager: The Poetic Development of Wallace Stevens* (New York: Oxford Univ. Press, 1972). "Infernale" appears in the *Letters,* p. 285, as "The Guide of Alcestis," with variants noted.

2. Louise (Norton) Varèse, Interview with the author, December 18, 1978.

3. Donald Evans to Carl Van Vechten, August 14 (or 13?), 1913, in the Carl Van Vechten collection of the Beinecke Rare Book Library of Yale University. Rpt. in Van Vechten, "The Origin of the Sonnets from the Patagonian," Annotated and with an introduction by Bruce Kellner, *Hartwick Review,* Vol. 3, No. 1 (Spring 1967), p. 56.

4. Stevens used a similar pseudonym in his first poems published in *Poetry* (Sept. 1914): "Phases" was signed "Peter Parasol." This early application of the dandy-persona to a series of war poems anticipates Stevens's later interest in the soldier/poet in "Lettres d'un Soldat" and in "Notes toward a Supreme Fiction." See chap. 4.

5. Van Vechten describes his first meeting with Wallace Stevens, on Saturday, November 21, 1914, in "Rogue Elephant in Porcelain," *Yale University Library Gazette,* Vol. 38, No. 2 (October 1963), pp. 41-50. Stevens did not meet the other "Patagonians" till several weeks later, through the machination of Van Vechten.

6. Van Vechten, cover note to Donald Evans material in the Carl Van Vechten Collection of the Beinecke Library, dated February 13, 1955.

7. Donald Evans's diary (March 31, 1904-June 14, 1905) records his determination to become a poet; the original of this document resides in the John Hay Library of Brown University. I am indebted to the Registrar of Haverford College for the date of Evans's withdrawal from college.

8. The Harvard University Archives provided information about Allen Norton's brief career at Harvard.

9. Louise Varèse, interview.

10. Mabel Dodge Luhan, *Movers and Shakers, Volume Three of Intimate Memoirs* (New York: Harcourt, Brace, 1936), pp. 15-16.

11. Van Vechten uses this phrase to describe his role in the imaginary "post-decadent" movement, which was to involve the same group of people, in "Rogue Elephant." The phrase accurately describes his role as social commentator on literary affairs.

12. Van Vechten, *Peter Whiffle: His Life and Works* (New York: Knopf, 1922), pp. 123-24.

13. Donald Evans to Carl Van Vechten, January 27, 1914, in the Carl Van Vechten Collection of the Beinecke Library.

14. Van Vechten, "Origin of the Sonnets from the Patagonian," pp. 51-53.

15. Mable Dodge makes this connection explicit in her "Speculations," *Camera Work, "Special Number"* (June 1913), pp. 6-9: "... Gertrude Stein is doing with words what Picasso is doing with paint." (p. 6)

16. *Camera Work, "Special Number"* (June 1913), pp. 3-5.

17. Dodge, "Speculations," p. 7.

18. Van Vechten, "Origin...," p. 53.

19. Arthur Davison Ficke to Donald Evans, May 18, 1916, in the Houghton Library, Harvard University.

20. Van Vechten, cover note to Donald Evans material at Beinecke. Kenneth Fields argues that most of Evans's sonnets are autobiographical in "Past Masters: Walter Conrad Arensberg and Donald Evans," *Southern Review*, Vol. VI, n.s., No. 2 (April, 1970), pp. 317-39.

21. Bruce Kellner, *Carl Van Vechten and the Irreverent Decades* (Norman: Univ. of Oklahoma Press, 1968), p. 71.

22. Lloyd R. Morris, *The Young Idea: An Anthology of Opinion Concerning the Spirit and Aims of Contemporary American Literature* (New York: Duffield & Co., 1917), pp. 19-20.

23. *Poetry*, Vol. V, No. 1 (October 1914), pp. 41-42.

24. Amy Lowell to Donald Evans, June 7, 1918, in the Houghton Library of Harvard University. Printed in S. Foster Damon, *Amy Lowell: A Chronicle* (Boston: Houghton Mifflin Co., 1935), pp. 458-59.

25. Leona Leonard, "Green Orchids and Purple Philosophy," *New York Morning Telegraph*, Sunday, March 1, 1914.

26. Howard Willard Cook, *Our Poets of Today* (New York: Moffatt, Yard & Co., 1918), p. 137.

27. Van Vechten, "Rogue Elephant," p. 49.

28. *Rogue*, I.i (March 15, 1915), p. 12.

29. Buttel discusses Stevens's college verse in "Part of his Education," pp. 3-45.

30. Litz, p. 12.

31. *The Collected Poems of W.B. Yeats* (New York: Macmillan, 1933, 1976), p. 102.

32. "The Tragic Generation" is reprinted in Yeats's *Autobiography* as part of the section entitled "The Trembling of the Veil" (1922).

33. Richard Ellmann made this point in a lecture on "The Decadents" at Princeton University in the spring of 1980.

34. Richard Ellmann, *Yeats: The Man and the Masks* (New York: Norton, 1948, 1979), pp. 214-17.

35.   Ezra Pound, "The Later Yeats," *Poetry,* IV.ii. (May 1914), pp. 64-9.

36.   Ibid., p. 67.

37.   W.B. Yeats, *Poems, 1899-1905* (London: A.H. Bullen, 1906), p. xii.

38.   In the Stevens Collection at the Huntington Library there is a letter from Elizabeth Yeats to Wallace Stevens, written on "Cuala Industries" stationery, and dated September 19, 1914. She encloses their circulars, "as requested."

39.   *TLS,* Daniel Traister, Rare Books Librarian of the New York Public Library, to the author April 30, 1980. The Cuala Press edition of *Responsibilities* was published on May 25, 1914, according to Allan Wade, *A Bibliography of the Writings of W.B. Yeats* (London: Rupert Hart-Davis, 1951).

40.   W.B. Yeats, *Responsibilities and Other Poems* (Cuala Press, 1914). This note was retained through all the editions of his poems. See the *Collected Poems,* p. 452.

41.   Ellman, *Yeats,* p. 211.

42.   Yeats, *Collected Poems,* p. 155; A Norman Jeffares, *A Commentary on the Collected Poems of W.B. Yeats* (Stanford: Stanford Univ. Press, 1968), p. 162.

43.   Buttel, p. 186.

44.   The OED lists this meaning at least as early as the nineteenth century. It is interesting to note that Stevens saw a play called "The Doll Girl" in August of 1913: ALS, WS to Elsie, August 28, 1913, in the Huntington Library.

45.   Harriet Monroe to WS, January 27, 1915. Rpt. Buttel, 187.

46.   Buttel, pp. 185-86.

47.   Alfred Kreymborg, *Our Singing Strength: An Outline of American Poetry (1620-1930),* (New York: Coward-McCann, 1929), p. 407.

48.   Edward Lueders, *Carl Van Vechten* (New York: Twayne, 1965), p. 34.

Chapter 2

1.   *TLS,* Wallace Stevens to Ferdinand Reyher, February 2, 1922. Unpublished letter in the McKeldin Library of the University of Maryland. Reyher was a writer-friend of Stevens, and later a friend of Bertolt Brecht. For a biography, see James K. Lyon, *Bertolt Brecht's American Cicerone* (Bonn, 1978).

2.   Ferdinand Earle, ed. *The Lyric Year: One Hundred Poems* (New York: Mitchell Kennerley, 1912), p. viii.

3.   For a good survey of Stieglitz and the New York avant-garde, see Bram Dijkstra, *The Hieroglyphics of a New Speech: Cubism, Stieglitz, and the Early Poetry of William Carlos Williams* (Princeton Univ. Press, 1969), pp. 3-46.

4.   Milton W. Brown, *American Painting from the Armory Show to the Depression* (Princeton: Princeton Univ. Press, 1955), p. 47. For a detailed history, see his *The Story of the Armory Show* (Joseph Hirshhorn Foundation; distributed by New York Graphic Society, Greenwich, Conn., 1963).

5.   The best studies of Wallace Stevens and painting are: Michael Benamou, *Wallace Stevens and the Symbolist Imagination* (Princeton: Princeton Univ. Press, 1972), "Poetry and Painting," pp. 1-24; Robert Buttel, *Wallace Stevens: The Making of Harmonium* (Princeton:

Princeton Univ. Press, 1967), "A Clinging Eye," pp. 148-68; James Baird, *The Dome and the Rock: Structure in the Poetry of Wallace Stevens* (Baltimore: Johns Hopkins Press, 1968), passim, but especially "The Painter: Encounters of the Eye," p. 167-92; and Kathleen Petrisky Weiss, *The Fundamental Aesthetic: Wallace Stevens and the Painters* (Ph.D. thesis, Univ. of Massachusetts, 1975).

6.   *L,* 850.

7.   This letter is quoted extensively in Fiske Kimball, "Cubism and the Arensberg," *Art News Annual,* xxiv (1954), pp. 117-22, 174-78; and reprinted in full in Stevens's *Letters,* pp. 820-23. All the letters about Arensberg which Fiske Kimball solicited in 1954 are now located in the Arensberg Archives of the Philadelphia Museum of Art. I wish to thank Anne d'Harnoncourt and Marge Kline of the Museum for allowing me access to this material, and for their kind assistance during the course of my research.

8.   When the Philadelphia Museum of Art was urging Arensberg to donate his collection, one of the appeals Fiske Kimball used was that the collection ought to be housed in Arensberg's home state. All correspondence concerning the Arensberg collection is in the Arensberg Archives at the Museum.

9.   Stevens's courses are listed in the *Letters,* pp. 23 and 33; for the information concerning Arensberg's courses I am indebted to Francis Naumann and the Registrar of Harvard University.

10.   *SP,* 37.

11.   The two sonnets published in the *Harvard Monthly* were signed "John Morris 2nd" (July 1899), and "Hilary Harness" (December 1899). Both are reprinted in Buttel, pp. 12-13.

12.   *L,* 482.

13.   *The Divine Comedy of Dante Alighieri,* translated by Charles Eliot Norton (Boston: Houghton Mifflin, 1891, 1892, 1902). Three volumes.

14.   Arensberg published his interpretation of Dante in *The Cryptography of Dante* (New York: Knopf, 1921); his unpublished translation of the *Divine Comedy* has disappeared, according to Elizabeth S. Wrigley, Curator of the Francis Bacon Library in Claremont, California.

15.   Francis Naumann, "Walter Conrad Arensberg: Poet, Patron, and Participant in the New York Avant-Garde, 1914-1920," *Philadelphia Museum of Art Bulletin,* Vol. 76, No. 328 (Spring 1980), pp. 1-32.

16.   Of Arensberg and Sanborn, Stevens tells us, "They remained friends throughout their lives" (*L,* 821). Stevens and Sanborn kept in touch regularly throughout their lives, too. The last letter at the Huntington from Sanborn to Stevens is dated February 18, 1941. Sanborn died on March 8, 1941.

17.   These dates are not exact. Arensberg moved to New York sometime in 1914 or early 1915. He and his wife visited California for an extended period in 1921, but their names are listed in the New York Telephone Directory through 1923. See Naumann, "Cryptography and the Arensberg Circle," *Arts Magazine,* Vol. 51, No. 9 (May, 1977), p. 132.

18.   Katherine Kuh, "Walter Arensberg and Marcel Duchamp," *Saturday Review,* September 5, 1970, pp. 36-37, 58. Rpt. in her *The Open Eye: In Pursuit of Art* (New York: Harper and Row, 1971), pp. 56-64.

19.   Walter Pach recalls these conversations in an unpublished manuscript entitled, "The Politer, the Cutt'n'er," now located in the Arensberg Archives of the Philadelphia Museum of Art. Cited by Naumann in "Walter Conrad Arensberg," p. 7.

20. Stevens's contributions to the *Modern School* were: "Earthy Anecdote," illustrated by Walter Pach (July 1918); "Moment of Light," a translation of "Instant de Clarte," by Jean le Roy, also illustrated by Walter Pach (October 1918); and "The Apostrophe to Vincentine," illustrated by Rockwell Kent (December 1918). Carl Zigrosser, once an English teacher at the Ferrer School, and the editor of *Modern School,* recalls his acquaintance with Stevens in his *My Own Shall Come to Me: A Personal Memoir and Picture Chronicle* (Casa Laura, 1971), pp. 79-84.

21. Among the distinctly Cubist works displayed in the Arensberg apartment in 1918, there were 5 Braques, 4 Picassos, 6 Duchamps, and 1 Picabia. See Naumann, "Walter Conrad Arensberg," pp. 8-10.

22. On Stevens and Cubism, see Benamou, pp. 1-24; Buttel, pp. 80, 81, 163-65; and Wylie Sypher, *Rococo to Cubism in Art and Literature* (New York: Random House, 1960), pp. 259, 318-21.

23. See Alfred Kreymborg, *Troubadour: An Autobiography* (New York: Boni and Liveright, 1925), pp. 238-45; 330-35; 360. See also Mabel Dodge Luhan, *Movers and Shakers, Volume Three of Intimate Memoirs* (New York: Harcourt, Brace, 1936).

24. Dijkstra, *Hieroglyphics;* Dickran Tishjian, *Skyscraper Primitives: Dada and the American Avant-Garde: 1910-1925* (Middletown, Conn.: Wesleyan Univ. Press, 1975).

25. Kreymborg, p. 219.

26. Ibid., p. 220.

27. In an interview with the author on December 18, 1978, Louise (Norton) Varèse commented on her relationship with Alfred Kreymborg, and said that she met Stevens only once, at Walter Arensberg's. Kreymborg describes the party with Stevens and Moore in *Troubadour,* pp. 330-35; and Stevens writes that he never met Moore until 1945 in *L,* 457.

28. Van Vechten, "Rogue Elephant," p. 43.

29. *Rogue* I.3 (April 15, 1915), p. 15.

30. James Abbott McNeill Whistler, *The Gentle Art of Making Enemies* (London: Heineman, 1890), pp. 131-59. I wish to thank Bruce Gardiner for bringing this book to my attention.

31. Ibid., pp. 158-59.

32. David Gray's "In the Shadows: A Poem in Sonnets," is reprinted in *Bibelot,* Vol. 6 (Portland, Maine: T.B. Mosher, 1900), pp. 181-214. Stevens's journal entry is printed in *L,* 46; and rpt. in *SP,* 84.

33. Hoffman, Frederick J., Charles Allen, and Carolyn F. Ulrich, *The Little Magazine: A History and Bibliography* (Princeton: Princeton University Press, 1946). The entry for *Rogue* is on p. 248, and lists only the March 15—September 15, 1915, issues.

34. *Rogue,* III.1 (October 1916), p. 2.

35. Naumann, "Walter Conrad Arensberg," p. 17.

36. Carl Van Vechten, Pitts Sanborn, and John Covert all record their flights from Europe at the outbreak of World War I in the pages of *Trend:* October, 1914 (CVV, pp. 13-24; PS, pp. 39-55) and November, 1914 (CVV, pp. 146-52; JC, pp. 204-10).

37. William Carlos Williams, *The Autobiography of William Carlos Williams* (New York: New Directions, 1951), p. 137.

38. *L,* 699, 792, 185.

39. William Innes Homer and Louise Hassett Lincoln, "New York Dada and the Arensberg Circle," in William Innes Homer, *Alfred Stieglitz and the American Avant-Garde* (Boston: New York Graphic Society, 1977), p. 184.

40. This picture is reproduced in Tashjian, between pages 90 and 91.

41. Naumann, "Walter Conrad Arensberg," p. 4; the quotation about "wordy battles" below is also taken from this article, p. 4.

42. Katherine Kuh, "Walter Arensberg and Marcel Duchamp," p. 36.

43. Homer, p. 185.

44. Holly Stevens, letter to the author, November 19, 1979.

45. *TLS,* William M. Ivins, Jr., to Fiske Kimball, March 15, 1954. Arensberg Archives, Philadelphia Museum of Art.

46. Kreymborg, p. 220.

47. Ibid.

48. Ivins, *TLS* cited above; Fiske Kimball prints an edited version of this quotation in "Cubism and the Arensbergs."

49. Naumann, "Cryptography and the Arensberg Circle," p. 132 (fn. 8).

50. Arensberg's books on the Bacon controversy are: *The Cryptography of Shakespeare* (1921); *The Secret Grave of Francis Bacon at Lichfield* (1923); *The Baconian Keys* (1928); *The Shakespearean Mystery* (1928); *Francis Bacon, William Butts, and the Pagets of Beaudesert* (1929); and *The Magic Ring of Francis Bacon* (1930).

51. Naumann, "Cryptography and the Arensberg Circle," pp. 127-33.

52. *The Cryptography of Dante,* p. 11.

53. *OP,* 171. The same sentence reappears in the poem, "Man Carrying Thing," (*CP,* 350).

54. *The Cryptography of Dante,* pp. 10-11; quoted by Naumann in "Cryptography and the Arensberg Circle," p. 128.

55. I follow the transcription in the *Commemorative Issue* of the *Wallace Stevens Journal,* Vol. 3, No. 3 and 4 (Fall 1979), p. 71, except that I read "lure" instead of "leer" in line 15. Phrases in brackets are legible erasures. Cf. Buttel, pp. 187-88.

56. Litz, *Introspective Voyager,* p. 28.

57. Kuh, p. 58.

58. Man Ray and Arturo Schwarz, "An Interview with Man Ray: 'This is Not for America,'" *Arts Magazine,* Vol. 51, No. 9 (May 1977), p. 119.

59. Quoted in Naumann, "The Big Show: The First Exhibition of the Society of Independent Artists," *Artforum* (April 1979), p. 52.

60. Arturo Schwarz, *Marcel Duchamp* (New York: Abrams, 1975), quoted from the introduction which is unpaginated.

61. Anne d'Harnoncourt and Kynaston McShine, eds. *Marcel Duchamp* (n.p., The Museum of Modern Art and Philadelphia Museum of Art, 1973), p. 249.

62. Brown, *American Painting,* p. 111.

63. *L,* 297.

64. d'Harnoncourt and McShine, p. 260.

65. Joseph Riddel, *The Clairvoyant Eye: The Poetry and Poetics of Wallace Stevens* (Baton Rouge: Louisiana State Univ. Press, 1965), p. 65.

66. The factual details of this paragraph are taken from Naumann, "Walter Conrad Arensberg."

67. *L,* 185.

68. Samuel French Morse, *Wallace Stevens: Poetry as Life* (New York: Pegasus, 1970), p. 69.

69. For a discussion of Duchamp's years in New York, see Moira Roth, "Marcel Duchamp in America: A Self Ready-Made," *Arts Magazine,* Vol. 51, No. 9 (May 1977) pp. 92-96.

70. *TLS,* Pitts Sanborn to Wallace Stevens, May 23, 1917. In the Huntington Library, San Marino, California: "I am sending you a copy of the Blind Man for May in case you have not seen it. It is not for sale. Carl V.V. got me several copies and tells me Mrs. Harry Payne Whitney paid for the publication of this number—the second—provided it should not be offered for sale. The contents are variously interesting."

71. d'Harnoncourt and McShine, p. 272.

72. *291,* Nos. 5-6, (July-August, 1915).

73. For a detailed discussion of the *Large Glass,* using Duchamp's own notes for its construction, see Richard Hamilton, "The Large Glass," in d'Harnoncourt and McShine, pp. 57-68.

74. Tashjian, p. 54.

75. Arturo Schwarz, unpaginated introduction.

76. Kuh, "Walter Arensberg and Marcel Duchamp," p. 37.

77. *Blindman,* No. 2 (May, 1917), p. 6.

78. Ibid., p. 5.

79. Robert Motherwell, ed., *The Dada Painters and Poets: An Anthology* (New York: Wittenborn, Schultz, Inc., 1951), p. xvii.

80. Holly Stevens, "Flux^2," *Southern Review,* Vol. 15, No. 4 (October 1979), p. 77.

81. William Carlos Williams, *Imaginations,* edited with introductions by Webster Schott (New York: New Directions, 1970), p. 10.

82. Williams, *Collected Early Poems* (New York: New Directions, 1966), p. 277.

83. Tashjian, p. 108.

84. Williams, *Imaginations,* p. 14.

85. Moira Roth, p. 92.

Chapter 3

1. Arensberg's *Poems* (1914) and *Idols* (1916) were both in Stevens's library, now at the Huntington Library. See Milton J. Bates, "Stevens' Books at the Huntington: An Annotated Checklist," *Wallace Stevens Journal,* Vol. 2, No. 3-4 (Fall 1978), pp. 45-61.

2.   Hi Simons was the first to note this parallel, in "Wallace Stevens and Mallarmé," *Modern Philology*, XLII (May 1964), pp. 257-58. See also Buttel, pp. 95-96; and Fields, "Past Masters," pp. 322-24.

3.   Arensberg's Dada poems have recently been collected in Jerome Rothenberg's *Revolution of the Word* (New York: Seabury, 1974). They are:

> "Ing," *Rogue* III.3 (December 1916), p. 4.
> "Axiom," *Blind Man*, No. 2 (May 1917), p. 8.
> "Theorem," *Blind Man*, No. 2 (May 1917), p. 9.
> "Arithmetical Progression of the Verb 'To Be'," *391*, No. 5 (June 1917), p. 1.
> "For 'Shady Hill,' Cambridge, Mass," *391*, No. 5 (June 1917), p. 5.
> "Vacuum Tires: A Formula for the Digestion of Figments," *TNT* (March 1919).
> "Dada is American," *Littérature*, Vol. II, No. 13 (May 1920), pp. 15-16.

Since both "Vacuum Tires" and "Dada is American" are really prose (though, admittedly, such distinctions are hard to make in such cases), we may say that Arensberg published his last poem in 1917. "Dada is American" may not have been written by Arensberg at all. See Naumann, "The New York Dada Movement: Better Late Than Never," *Arts Magazine* (February 1980), p. 145.

4.   The manuscript of "Sonatina to Hans Christian" is described in Louis L. Martz, "Manuscripts of Wallace Stevens," *The Yale University Library Gazette*, Vol. 54, No. 2 (October 1979), p. 65. My own transcription of Stevens's manuscript differs from Martz's in one particular: line 13 of the "WCA Suggests" version reads "What of the might" where Martz has "What of the *night*". I have checked the manuscript again, and believe my transcription is the correct one.

     This manuscript helps us to date "Sonatina to Hans Christian." Since Arensberg made suggestions, the poem must have been written before the two men fought (in 1921), after which time Stevens "never saw him again" (*L*, 850). The poem may well have been written much earlier than usually assumed. If Arensberg lost interest in writing poetry in 1917, that may be the *latest* date we ought to assign to this poem.

5.   Ronald Sukenick, *Wallace Stevens: Musing the Obscure* (New York: New York Univ. Press, 1967), p. 228.

6.   Elizabeth S. Wrigley, Curator of the Francis Bacon Library which houses most of Arensberg's books and papers, assures me that Arensberg did translate all of the *Divine Comedy*, though the manuscript has since disappeared.

7.   Morse, *Wallace Stevens*, p. 77.

8.   *TLS*, William M. Ivins, Jr., to Fiske Kimball, March 15, 1954. Quoted in Kimball's "Cubism and the Arensbergs," *Art News Annual*, xxiv (1954), p. 177.

9.   Arensberg, *Idols*, p. 78.

10.   Arensberg, *The Cryptography of Dante* (New York: Knopf, 1921). Francis Naumann discusses Arensberg's interpretation of Dante in his "Cryptography and the Arensberg Circle," *Arts Magazine*, Vol. 51, No. 9 (May 1977), pp. 127-28.

11.   Arensberg, *Idols*, p. 76.

12.   Morse, *Wallace Stevens*, p. 76.

13.   Ibid., pp. 76-77; Litz, *Introspective Voyager*, pp. 52-53.

14.   The manuscript of "For an Old Woman in a Wig" is in the Wallace Stevens Collection of the Huntington Library in San Marino, California.

15. George Santayana, *Three Philosophical Poets: Lucretius, Dante, Goethe* (Cambridge, Harvard Univ. Press, 1910), pp. 118, 120.

16. *ALS,* WCW to WS, June 2, 1916, in the Huntington Library.

17. Williams's poem "Smell!" first appeared in *Poetry* in July, 1917.

Chapter 4

1. *Lettres d'un Soldat* (Août 1914-Avril 1915), *Preface de André Chevrillon* (Paris: Librairie Chapelot, 1916). All translations are taken from the translation by "V.M.," *Letters of a Soldier: 1914-1915, with an Introduction by A. Clutton-Brock and a Preface by André Chevrillon* (London: Constable, 1917). The letters were published anonymously, but for the sake of clarity I shall refer to Lemercier by name, and to the protagonist of Stevens's poems as "the soldier."

2. Litz, *Introspective Voyager.* All the extant poems from "Lettres" are printed in Appendix B.4, pp. 309-16. I follow Litz's numbering of these poems.

3. December 21, 1914. The date of the letter, rather than the page number, is given so that the reader may easily consult any edition of this book.

4. March 17, 1915.

5. Morse, "Lettres d'un Soldat," *Dartmouth College Library Bulletin,* 4 N.S. (December 1961), p. 49; Litz, *Introspective Voyager,* pp. 76-77.

6. March 15, 1915.

7. January 9, 1915.

8. The immediate impact of the First World War on Stevens and his friends is discussed in chap. 2, pp. 40-41.

9. For a discussion of the relation between the "Primordia" series and "Lettres," see Litz, *Introspective Voyager,* pp. 61-77.

10. April 3, 1915.

11. Paul Fussell, *The Great War and Modern Memory* (New York: Oxford, 1975), Chapter V, "Oh What a Literary War," pp. 155-90.

12. November 10, 1914.

13. January 22, 1914.

14. December 9, 1914.

15. November 29, 1914.

16. "Death was a reaper..." is numbered XVII in the manuscripts. See Litz, p. 309. "Lunar Paraphrase," Poem VII, was also cut, possibly because its "pathos and pity" seemed out of place in the more restrained edited version.

17. Fussell, p. 21.

18. April 5, 1915.

19. Fussell, p. 74.

20. Joseph Riddell: *The Clairvoyant Eye: The Poetry and Poetics of Wallace Stevens* (Baton Rouge: Louisiana Univ. Press, 1965), p. 162.

21.   *Palm,* p. 206.

22.   This reading of the epilogue to "Notes" dissents from the view of Helen Vendler who sees it as "something of an anticlimax." See her *On Extended Wings: Wallace Stevens' Longer Poems* (Cambridge, Harvard Univ. Press, 1969), p. 205.

Chapter 5

1.   *TLS,* WS to Ferdinand Reyher, June 1, 1921, in the McKeldin Library of the University of Maryland.

2.   DE met Robinson through Mabel Dodge (see her *Movers and Shakers,* p. 74); Louise (Norton) Varèse recalled that DE and EAR were friendly in the early 1910s (interview with the author, 12/18/78); and letters from EAR to A.D. Ficke in 1921 show that the friendship had continued till DE's death (the letters are dated 6/11/21 and 6/23/21, and are in the Houghton Library at Harvard University). Thanks to Wallace Anderson for bringing these letters to my attention.

     DE corresponded with Amy Lowell in 1917-18. She disliked his Patagonian manner, but concluded: "Whatever I may think of the subject matter of your 'Patagonian Sonnets,' I think they showed great talent for poetry. Nobody in reading them could deny that." (6/14/18) (The entire correspondence is in the Houghton Library at Harvard.)

     Ezra Pound included two of Evans's poems in his anthology, *Profile: An Anthology Collected in 1931* (Milan: John Scheiwiller, 1932).

3.   Paul Rosenfeld, "An American Sonneteer," *Dial,* Vol. 80 (March 1926), pp. 197-201; rpt. in his *By Way of Art* (New York: Coward-McCann, 1928); Kreymborg, *Troubadour,* p. 333; Witter Bynner's remarks are quoted from a transcript of a letter from Bynner to Michael Lafferty, dated June 1, 1959, in the personal files of Holly Stevens.

4.   Pitts Sanborn, *Vie de Bordeaux* (Philadelphia: Nicholas L. Brown, 1916.) The full dedication reads:

> TO
> Wallace Stevens
>   in gratitude
> Donald Evans
>   in reverence
> Walter Conrad Arensberg
>   an idol
> The Reverend Albert Parker Fitch
>   an image
> Carl Van Vechten
>   why not?
> Emily Latimer
>   her book
> AND
> Rose of the World
>
> FOR YOU

Arthur Davison Ficke's comment is in a *TLS* to S. Foster Damon, dated September 19, 1935, in the John Hay Library of Brown University.

     The Reverend Albert Parker Fitch left Harvard with Stevens and Sanborn (Class of 1900), and became a well-known minister and professor of religion. WS wrote to Elsie on

September 8, 1913: "Yesterday... I went to hear Albert Parker Fitch in the Brick Presbyterian Church. This man is one of the best preachers I ever heard; and, since he is to be here during September, I look forward to real elevation...." (Huntington Library). From 1909-17, Fitch was President of the Andover Theological Seminary in Cambridge, Mass.; from 1917-23 he was professor of the history of religion at Amherst College.

I cannot identify Emily Latimer. "Rose of the World" may refer to Yeats's poem of that title. But it seems possible, too, that it might be a pet name for Sanborn's friend, Rose O'Neill, who was an illustrator and the creator of the Kewpie Doll.

5. Kreymborg, *Our Singing Strength*, p. 408; Bynner, op. cit.; Samuel French Morse, *Wallace Stevens: Life as Poetry*, p. 111.

6. From the personal files of Holly Stevens.

7. Litz, "Particles of Order: The Unpublished Adagia," in Frank Doggett and Robert Buttel, eds., *Wallace Stevens: A Celebration* (Princeton: Princeton Univ. Press, 1980), pp. 30-45. See also: George S. Lensing, "*From Pieces of Paper:* A Wallace Stevens Notebook," *Southern Review*, Vol. 15, No. 4 (Oct. 1979), pp. 877-920.

8. Donald Evans's notebook is in the John Hay Library of Brown University.

9. Evans's journal is in the John Hay Library of Brown University. Typed or carbon copies of this journal, executed by A.D. Ficke, are in the Beinecke Library at Yale, and the Houghton Library at Harvard. *ALS*, DE to A.D. Ficke, February 27, 1921: "I am taking my first real holiday in 18 years, and I may spin it out till 1922 if I find I can do any poetry" (Houghton Library, Harvard).

10. Van Vechten, "Rogue Elephant," p. 43.

11. Van Vechten, cover note to DE material in the Carl Van Vechten collection of the Beinecke Library, dated February 13, 1955.

12. Louise Varèse, interviews with the author, December 18, 1978 and May 9, 1980.

13. A.D. Ficke, note about DE among the Harvard material.

14. *ALS*, Otto Frederick Theis to A.D. Ficke, December 28, 1921, at the Houghton Library, Harvard University. Theis was an old friend of Evans. He is mentioned in Evans's diary of 1904. He was an editor at DE's publisher, N.L. Brown Co.; he worked with DE on the Claire Marie Press; and later, in 1921, he moved to London, became a British citizen, and worked in publishing there.

15. Amy Lowell criticized DE for posing: "I detest pose," *TLS*, AL to DE, June 7, 1918. Printed in S. Foster Damon, *Amy Lowell: A Chronicle* (Boston: Houghton Mifflin Co., 1935), pp. 458-59. In her "A Critical Fable," she writes of Stevens: "He has published no book and adopts this as pose," and makes this the essence of her character-sketch.

16. *ALS*, DE to A.D. Ficke, June 13, 1916, in the Houghton Library, Harvard.

17. Louise Varèse, interview with the author, December 18, 1978.

18. Kreymborg, *Troubadour*, pp. 333-34.

19. Richard Le Gallienne, *The Romantic Nineties*. (Garden City, New York: Doubleday, Page & Co., 1925), p. 269. His full description of Wilde is worth quoting: "He (Wilde) is, beyond comparison, the incarnation of the spirit of the '90s. The significance of the '90s is that they began to apply all the new ideas that had been for some time accumulating from the disintegrating action of scientific and philosophic thought on every kind of spiritual, moral,

social, and artistic convention, and all forms of authority demanding obedience merely as authority.... Wilde was the synthesis of all these phenomena of change. He may be said to have included Huxley and Pater and Morris and Whistler and Mr. Bernard Shaw and Mr. Max Beerbohm in the amazing eclecticism of his extravagant personality, that seems to have borrowed everything and made everything his own. Out of the 1890 chaos he emerged an astonishing, impudent microcosm."

20. Donald Evans's Journal, John Hay Library, Brown University. The entry is dated April 10, 1904.

21. *Discords* (Philadelphia: N.L. Brown, 1912), p. 112. Kenneth Fields remarks on this connection in his "Past Masters: Walter Conrad Arensberg and Donald Evans," op. cit.
    Oscar Wilde was a cult hero of the Patagonians generally. Carl Van Vechten alludes to him frequently in criticism from this period, defending his achievement against his fallen reputation. Allen Norton devotes four of the *Saloon Sonnets* to Wilde.

22. Page numbers refer to the 1914 edition (Claire Marie).

23. Wilde addresses sonnets to Sarah Bernhardt and Ellen Terry in *The Complete Works of Oscar Wilde*, with an Introduction by Vyvyan Holland (London: Collins, 1948, 1973), pp. 777-78. Donald Evans dedicates sonnets to the actresses Fania Marinoff (11, 23, 35), Claire Burke (27, 35), and Leah Winslow (DE's first wife, and the "Mme. Hyssain" of the *Sonnets* according to A.D. Ficke) (27).

24. For the best discussion of the significance of the figure of the dandy/aesthete in Stevens's early poetry, see Milton James Bates, *Wallace Stevens: The Pursuit of Mastery* (Ph.D. dissertation, Berkeley, 1977).

25. Quoted by Daniel Fuchs in *The Comic Spirit of Wallace Stevens* (Durham, N.C.: Duke Univ. Press, 1963), p. 6.

26. Quoted from the 1918 edition of *Sonnets from the Patagonian*, unpaginated Preface.

27. Quoted by Richard Ellmann in "The Critic as Artist as Wilde," from *Wilde and the Nineties: An Essay and an Exhibition*, edited by Charles Ryskamp (Princeton: Princeton Univ. Library, 1966), p. 10.

28. The United States declared war on April 6, 1917. Evans enlisted on June 21, 1917. (This information was supplied by the National Personnel Records Center of the United States General Services Administration.) Evans never made it overseas.

29. Buttel, p. 83.

30. *The Complete Works of Oscar Wilde*, p. 788.

31. Vendler, *On Extended Wings*, p. 58.

32. Litz, *Introspective Voyager*, p. 84.

33. W.B. Yeats, *Autobiography* (New York; Macmillan, 1916, 1965), p. 190. Apparently Stevens, too, thought of "Hélas!" as the quintessence of Wilde, judging from this passage in his *Letters:* "... Until quite lately a group of nuns came [to the park] each morning to paint water colors especially of the water lilies. Whenever I saw them I thought of the chasteness of the girl in Oscar Wilde who spent her time looking at photographs of the Alps. But this morning even these exquisite creatures were no longer there and in addition the tops of the ferns were dry and there were acorns on the path. Hélas! Hélas! Hélas!..." (*L*, 610)

34. Ellmann, p. 6.

Chapter 6

1. The manuscript is in the Beinecke Rare Book Library at Yale. See Martz, "Manuscripts of Wallace Stevens," p. 61.

2. *TLS*, WCW to WS, June 8, 1916, in the Wallace Stevens Collection of the Huntington Library, San Marino, California. Rpt. in Buttel, op. cit., p. 190.

3. Buttel, p. 190.

4. Donald Gallup, "T.S. Eliot and Ezra Pound: Collaborators in Letters," *Poetry Australia*, 32 (1970), p. 67.

5. Ibid., p. 65.

6. Hugh Kenner, *A Homemade World* (New York: Knopf, 1975), p. 55. Jack Hardie seconds this notion in his "Hibiscus and the Spaniard of the Rose: Williams' Dialogue with Wallace Stevens," *William Carlos Williams Newsletter*, Vol. IV, No. 2 (Fall 1978), p. 23-24.

7. Williams, *Selected Essays* (New York: Random House, 1954), p. xii.

8. Williams, *Imaginations* (New York: New Directions, 1970), p. 14.

9. Ibid., p. 17.

10. Review of *The Man with the Blue Guitar* in *New Republic*, November 17, 1937, p. 50; *Harvard Advocate*, "Wallace Stevens Number," Vol. 127, No. 3, p. 32; "Wallace Stevens," *Poetry*, Vol. 87, No. 4 (January, 1956), p. 236.

11. Buttel, pp. 143-44.

12. Ibid.

13. Litz, *Introspective Voyager*, p. 57.

14. James Breslin, *William Carlos Williams: An American Artist* (New York: Oxford U.P., 1970), p. 25.

15. Williams, *I Wanted to Write a Poem: The Autobiography of the Works of a Poet*, reported and edited by Edith Heal (New York: New Directions, 1958), p. 23.

16. Hardie; Roger S. Mitchell, "Wallace Stevens' 'Spaniard of the Rose': William Carlos Williams," *Notes and Queries*, n.s. 10 (October 1961), pp. 381-82.

17. *Contact*, No. 1, December, 1920.

18. *TLS*, WS to Ferdinand Reyher, January 31, 1921, in the McKeldin Library of the University of Maryland.

19. WS to Harriet Monroe, January 30, 1921, in the Carl Sandburg Collection of the University of Illinois at Urbana-Champaign. Rpt. in the *Wallace Stevens Journal*, Vol. 2, No. 3 and 4 (Fall 1978), p. 19.

20. *TLS*, WS to Alfred Kreymborg, January 24, 1922, in the Loeb Collection, Rare Book Room, Princeton University Library.

21. Ezra Pound, *The Spirit of Romance* (London, 1952), p. 14. Quoted by Litz, *Introspective Voyager*, p. 103.

22. *Imaginations*, p. 112.

23. Ibid., p. 110.

24. Joseph N. Riddel, "The Wanderer and the Dance: William Carlos Williams' Early Poetics," in *The Shaken Realist: Essays in Modern Literature in Honor of Frederick J. Hoffman,* edited by Melvin J. Friedman and John B. Vickery (Baton Rouge: Louisiana State Univ. Press, 1970), p. 66.

25. *I Wanted to Write a Poem,* p. 52.

26. Ibid.

27. *Imaginations,* p. 88.

28. Ibid., p. 89.

29. The unfortunate influence of Stevens's Preface on subsequent criticism is remarked by Vivienne Koch in *William Carlos Williams* (New York: New Directions, 1950), pp. 60-62.

Bibliography

General Background (History and Literature)

Aaron, Daniel. *Men of Good Hope: A Story of American Progressives.* New York: Oxford Univ. Press, 1951.

Aiken, Conrad. *Skepticisms: Notes on Contemporary Poetry.* New York: Knopf, 1919.

Anderson, Margaret. *My Thirty Years' War.* New York: Covici-Friede, 1930.

Brooks, Van Wyck. *The Confident Years: 1885-1915.* New York: Dutton, 1955.

Coffman, Stanley K., Jr. *Imagism: A Chapter for the History of Modern Poetry.* Norman: University of Oklahoma Press, 1951.

Earnest, Ernest. *The Single Vision: The Alienation of American Intellectuals, 1910-1930.* New York: New York Univ. Press, 1970.

Edmiston, Susan and Linda D. Cirino. *Literary New York: A History and Guide.* Boston: Houghton Mifflin, 1976.

Fussell, Paul. *The Great War and Modern Memory.* New York: Oxford Univ. Press, 1975.

Hoffman, Frederick J., Charles Allen and Carolyn F. Ulrich, *The Little Magazine: A History and Bibliography.* Princeton: Princeton Univ. Press, 1946.

Hofstadter, Richard, ed. *The Progressive Movement: 1900-1915.* Englewood Cliffs, N.J.: Prentice-Hall, 1963.

Howarth, Herbert. *Notes on Some Figures Behind T.S. Eliot.* Boston: Houghton Mifflin, 1964.

Josephson, Matthew. *Life Among the Surrealists.* New York: Holt, Rinehart and Winston, 1962.

Kennedy, David M. *Over Here: The First World War and American Society.* New York: Oxford Univ. Press, 1980.

Kenner, Hugh. *The Pound Era.* Berkeley: Univ. of California Press, 1971.

Kreymborg, Alfred. *Troubador: An Autobiography.* New York: Boni and Liveright, 1925.

Link, Arthur S. *Woodrow Wilson and the Progressive Era: 1910-1917.* New York: Harper and Row, 1954.

Loeb, Harold. *The Way It Was.* New York: 1962.

Luhan, Mabel Dodge. *Movers and Shakers: Volume Three of Intimate Memoirs.* New York: Harcourt, Brace, 1936.

May, Henry F. *The End of American Innocence: A Study of the First Years of Our Own Time: 1913-1917.* London: Jonathan Cape, 1959.

Miller, James E., Jr. *The American Quest for a Supreme Fiction: Whitman's Legacy in the Personal Epic.* Chicago: Univ. of Chicago Press, 1979.

Pearce, Roy Harvey. *The Continuity of American Poetry.* Princeton: Princeton Univ. Press, 1961.

Perkins, David. *A History of Modern Poetry: From the 1890s to the High Modernist Mode.* Cambridge: Harvard Univ. Press, 1976.

Taupin, Rene. *L'Influence du Symbolisme Français sur La Poésie Americaine (de 1910 à 1920).* Paris: 1929.

Wertheim, Arthur Frank. *The New York Little Renaissance: Iconoclasm, Modernism, and Nationalism in American Culture, 1908-1917.* New York: New York Univ. Press, 1976.

Wallace Stevens

The Collected Poems of Wallace Stevens. New York: Knopf, 1954.

Letters of Wallace Stevens, selected and edited by Holly Stevens. New York: Knopf, 1966.

The Necessary Angel: Essays on Reality and the Imagination. New York: Knopf, 1951.

Opus Posthumous, ed. Samuel French Morse. New York: Knopf, 1957.

The Palm at the end of the Mind: Selected Poems and a Play by Wallace Stevens, ed. Holly Stevens. New York: Knopf, 1971; Vintage, 1972.

Holly Stevens, *Souvenirs and Prophecies: The Young Wallace Stevens.* New York: Knopf, 1977. [Contains Stevens's complete journal.]

Books about Wallace Stevens

Abernathy, William M., Jr. *The Swan and the Blackbird: A Comparison of the Poetic Figures of Stephane Mallarmé and Wallace Stevens.* Ph.D. dissertation, Princeton, 1976.

Baird, James. *The Dome and the Rock: Structure in the Poetry of Wallace Stevens.* Baltimore: Johns Hopkins Press, 1968.

Bates, Milton J. *Wallace Stevens: The Pursuit of Mastery.* Ph.D. dissertation, Berkeley, 1977.

Benamou, Michel. *Wallace Stevens and the Symbolist Imagination.* Princeton: Princeton Univ. Press, 1972.

Berger, Charles Stewart. *The Early and Middle Poetry of Wallace Stevens.* Ph.D. dissertation, Yale, 1977.

Blessing, Richard Allen. *Wallace Stevens' "Whole Harmonium."* Syracuse: Syracuse Univ. Press, 1970.

Bloom, Harold, *Wallace Stevens: The Poems of Our Climate.* Ithaca: Cornell Univ. Press, 1977.

Brown, Ashley and Robert S. Haller, eds. *The Achievement of Wallace Stevens.* New York: Lippincott, 1962.

Brown, Merle E. *Wallace Stevens: The Poem as Act.* Detroit: Wayne State Univ. Press, 1970.

Burney, William. *Wallace Stevens.* New York: Twayne, 1968.

Buttel, Robert. *Wallace Stevens: The Making of Harmonium.* Princeton: Princeton Univ. Press, 1967.

Doggett, Frank. *Stevens' Poetry of Thought.* Baltimore: Johns Hopkins Press, 1966

————. *Wallace Stevens: The Making of the Poem.* Baltimore: Johns Hopkins Press, 1980.

————. and Robert Buttel, eds. *Wallace Stevens: A Celebration.* Princeton: Princeton Univ. Press, 1980.

Edelstein, J.M. *Wallace Stevens: A Descriptive Bibliography.* Pittsburgh: Univ of Pittsburgh Press, 1973.

Enck, John J. *Wallace Stevens: Images and Judgements,* with a Preface by Harry T. Moore. Carbondale: Southern Illinois Univ. Press, 1964.

Fields, Kenneth Wayne. *The Rhetoric of Artifice: Ezra Pound, T.S. Eliot, Wallace Stevens, Walter Conrad Arensberg, Donald Evans, Mina Loy, and Yvor Winters.* Ph.D. dissertation, Stanford, 1967.

Fuchs, Daniel. *The Comic Spirit of Wallace Stevens.* Durham, North Carolina: Duke Univ. Press, 1963.

Kermode, Frank. *Wallace Stevens.* London: Oliver and Boyd, 1960.

Kessler, Edward. *Images of Wallace Stevens.* New Brunswick: Rutgers Univ. Press, 1972.

Lentricchia, Frank. *The Gaiety of Language: An Essay on the Radical Poetics of W.B. Yeats and Wallace Stevens.* Berkeley and Los Angeles: Univ. of California Press, 1968.

Litz, A. Walton. *Introspective Voyager: The Poetic Development of Wallace Stevens.* New York: Oxford Univ. Press, 1972.

Morris, Adalaide Kirby. *Wallace Stevens: Imagination and Faith.* Princeton: Princeton Univ. Press, 1974.

Morse, Samuel French. *Wallace Stevens: Poetry as Life.* New York: Pegasus, 1970.

O'Connor, William Van. *The Shaping Spirit: A Study of Wallace Stevens.* New York: Russell and Russell, 1964.

Pack, Robert. *Wallace Stevens: An Approach to His Poetry and Thought,* New Brunswick: Rutgers Univ. Press, 1958.

Pearce, Roy Harvey and J. Hillis Miller, eds. *An Act of the Mind: Essays on the Poetry of Wallace Stevens.* Baltimore: Johns Hopkins Press, 1965.

Perlis, Alan. *Wallace Stevens: A World of Transforming Shapes.* Lewisburg: Bucknell Univ. Press, 1976.

Ransom. James Clarence. *The Anecdotal Imagination: A Study of Wallace Stevens' Harmonium.* Ph.D. dissertation, Yale, 1969.

Ravitz, Martha Anne. *The Fabulous and Its Intrinsic Verse.* Ph.D. dissertation, Yale, 1978.

Riddel, Joseph N. *The Clairvoyant Eye: The Poetry and Poetics of Wallace Stevens.* Baton Rouge: Louisiana State Univ. Press, 1965.

Stern, Herbert J. *Wallace Stevens: Art of Uncertainty.* Ann Arbor: Univ. of Michigan Press, 1966.

Sukenick, Ronald. *Wallace Stevens: Musing the Obscure.* New York: New York Univ. Press, 1967.

Tindall, William York. *Wallace Stevens.* Minneapolis: Univ. of Minnesota Press, 1961.

Vendler, Helen Hennessy. *On Extended Wings: Wallace Stevens' Longer Poems.* Cambridge: Harvard Univ. Press, 1969.

Weiss, Kathleen Petrisky, *The Fundamental Aesthetic: Wallace Stevens and the Painters,* Ph.D. dissertation, Univ. of Massachusetts, 1975.

Weston, Susan B. *Wallace Stevens: An Introduction to the Poetry.* New York: Columbia Univ. Press, 1977.

Willard, Abbie F. *Wallace Stevens: The Poet and His Critics.* Chicago: American Library Association, 1978.

"The Patagonians"

Buck, Mitchell S. *Syrinx: Pastels of Hellas.* New York: Claire Marie, 1914.

Cook, Howard Willard. *Our Poets of Today.* New York: Moffatt, Yard & Co., 1918.

Dodge, Mabel "Speculations," *Camera Work: Special Number* (June 1913), pp. 6-9.

Ellmann, Richard, *Yeats: The Man and the Masks.* New York: Norton, 1948, 1979.

Evans, Donald. *Sonnets from the Patagonian: The Street of Little Hotels.* New York: Claire Marie, 1914.

Gallup, Donald, ed. *The Flowers of Friendship: Letters Written to Gertrude Stein.* New York: Knopf, 1953.

Jeffares, A. Norman. *A Commentary on the Collected Poems of W. B. Yeats.* Stanford: Stanford Univ. Press, 1968.

Kellner, Bruce. *Carl Van Vechten and the Irreverent Decades.* Norman: Univ of Oklahoma Press, 1968.

Lueders, Edward. *Carl Van Vechten.* New York: Twayne, 1965.

_____. *Carl Van Vechten and the Twenties.* Albuquerque: Univ. of New Mexico Press, 1955.

Mellow, James R. *Charmed Circle: Gertrude Stein and Company.* New York: Praeger, 1974.

Morris, Lloyd R. *The Young Idea: An Anthology of Opinion Concerning the Spirit and Aims of Contemporary American Literature.* New York: Duffield, 1917.

Norton, Allen. *The Convulvus: A Comedy in Three Acts.* New York: Claire Marie, 1914.

————. *Saloon Sonnets: With Sunday Flutings,* New York: Claire Marie, 1914.

Norton, Louise. *Little Wax Candle: A Farce in One Act.* New York: Claire Marie, 1914.

Stein Gertrude. *The Autobiography of Alice B. Toklas.* New York: Random House, 1933.

————. *Selected Writings of Gertrude Stein,* edited and with an introduction by Carl Van Vechten. New York: Random House, 1946.

————. *Tender Buttons: Objects, Food, Rooms.* New York: Claire Marie, 1914.

Sprigge, Elizabeth. *Gertrude Stein: Her Life and Work.* London: Hamish Hamilton, 1957.

Van Vechten, Carl. "How Donald Dedicated His Poem," *Rogue* 1.2, (April 1,1915), pp. 8-10.

————. *In The Garret.* New York: Knopf, 1919.

————. *Interpreters and Interpretations.* New York: Knopf, 1917.

————. *Music After the Great War and Other Studies. New York: G. Schirmer, 1915.*

————. *Music and Bad Manners.* New York: Knopf, 1916.

————. *The Music of Spain.* New York: Knopf, 1918.

————. *The Merry-Go-Round.* New York: Knopf, 1918.

————. "The Origin of the *Sonnets from the Patagonian,*" (annotated and with an Introduction by Bruce Kellner), *The Hartwick Review,* III.i (Spring 1967), pp. 50-56.

————. *Peter Whiffle: His Life and Works.* New York: Knopf, 1922.

————. "Rogue Elephant in Porcelain,' *The Yale University Library Gazette,* Vol. 38, No.2 (October, 1963), pp. 41-50.

————. *Sacred and Profane Memories.* New York: Knopf, 1932.

Varèse, Louise (Norton). *Varèse: A Looking-Glass Diary. Volume I: 1883-1928.* New York: Norton, 1972.

Yeats, William Butler. *The Autobiography of W.B. Yeats.* New York: Macmillan, 1916, 1965.

————. *The Collected Poems of W.B. Yeats.* New York: Macmillan, 1933.

————. *Poems: 1899-1905.* London: A.H. Bullen, 1906.

————. *Responsibilities and Other Poems.* Dublin: Cuala Press, 1914.

The "Art Crowd"

Arensberg, Walter Conrad. *The Baconian Keys.* Pittsburgh, 1928.

————. *The Burial of Francis Bacon and His Mother in the Lichfield Chapter House.* Pittsburgh, 1924.

————. *The Cryptography of Dante.* New York: Knopf, 1921.

————. *The Cryptography of Shakespeare.* Los Angeles: Howard Bowen, 1922.

————. *The Magic Ring of Francis Bacon.* Pittsburgh, 1930.

————. *The Secret Grave of Francis Bacon at Lichfield.* San Francisco: John Howell, 1925.

————. *The Shakespearian Mystery.* Pittsburgh, 1928.

Belz, Carl Irvin. *The Role of Man Ray in the Dada and Surrealist Movements.* Ph.D. dissertation, Princeton, 1963.

Brown, Milton W. *American Painting from the Armory Show to the Depression.* Princeton: Princeton Univ. Press, 1955.

————. *The Story of the Armory Show.* The Joseph Hirshhorn Foundation; distributed by the New York Graphic Society, 1963.

d'Harncourt, Anne and Kynaston McShine, eds. *Marcel Duchamp.* The Museum of Modern Art and the Philadelphic Museum of Art, 1973.

Dijkstra, Bram. *The Hieroglyphics of a New Speech: Cubism, Steiglitz, and the Early Poetry of William Carlos Williams.* Princeton: Princeton Univ. Press, 1969.

Dreier, Katherine. *Western Art and the New Era.* New York: Brentano's, 1923.

Guggenheim, Peggy. *Out of This Century.* New York: Dial, 1946.

Homer, William Inner. *Alfred Steiglitz and the American Avant-Garde.* Boston: New York Graphic Society, 1977.

Kimball, Fiske. "Cubism and the Arensbergs," *Art News Annual,* xxiv (1954), pp. 117-22.

Ko, Won. *Buddhist Elements in Dada: A Comparison of Tristan Trarza, Takahashi Shinkich, and Their Fellow Poets.* New York: New York Univ. Press, 1977.

Kuh, Katharine. *The Open Eye: In Pursuit of Art.* New York: Harper and Row, 1971.

Lippard, Lucy R. *Changing: Essays in Art Criticism.* New York: Dutton, 1971.

Motherwell, Robert, ed. *The Dada Painters and Poets: An Anthology.* New York: Wittenborn, Schultz, Inc., 1951.

Naumann, Francis. "The Big Show: The First Exhibition of the Society of Independent Artists," *Artforum,* (February, 1979), pp. 34-39; and (April, 1979), pp. 49-53.

_____. "Cryptography and the Arensberg Circle," *Arts Magazine,* Vol. 51, No. 9 (May, 1977), pp. 127-33.

_____. "The New York Dada Movement: Better Late Than Never," *Arts Magazine,* (February, 1980), pp. 143-49.

_____. "Walter Conrad Arensberg: Poet, Patron, and Participant in the New York Avant-Garde, 1914-1920," *The Philadelphia Museum of Art Bulletin,* Vol. 76, No. 328 (Spring 1980), pp. 1-32.

Ray, Man. *Self-Portrait.* Boston: Little, Brown, 1963.

_____. and Arturo Schwarz, "An Interview with Man Ray: 'This is not for America,'" *Arts Magzine,* Vol. 51, No. 9 (May, 1977), pp. 116-21.

Roth, Moira. "Marcel Duchamp in America: A Self Ready-Made," *Arts Magazine,* Vol. 51, No. 9 (May, 1977), pp. 92-96.

Schwarz, Arturo. *Marcel Duchamp.* New York: Abrams, 1975.

Sypher, Wylie. *Rococo to Cubism in Art and Literature.* New York: Random House, 1960.

Tashjian, Dickran. *Skyscraper Primitives: Dada and the American Avant-Garde, 1910-1925.* Middletown, Conn.: Wesleyan Univ. Press, 1975.

Whistler, James Abbot McNeill. *The Gentle Art of Making Enemies.* London: Heinemann, 1890.

Walter Conrad Arensberg

Arensberg, Walter Conrad. *Idols.* Boston: Hougton, Mifflin, 1916.

_____. *Poems.* Boston: Houghton, Mifflin, 1914.

Fields, Kenneth Wayne. "Past Masters: Walter Conrad Arensberg and Donald Evans," *Southern Review,* VI.2, n.s. (April, 1970), pp. 317-39.

Martz, Louis L. "Manuscripts of Wallace Stevens," *Yale University Library Gazette,* Vol. 54, No. 2 (October, 1979) pp. 51-67.

Rothenberg, Jerome, ed. *The Revolution of the Word: A New Gathering of American Avante-Garde Poetry, 1914-1945.* New York: Seabury, 1974.

Santayana, George. *Three Philosophical Poets: Lucretius, Dante, Goethe.* Cambridge: Harvard Univ. Press,, 1910.

Simons, Hi. "Wallace Stevens and Mallarmé," *Modern Philology,* XLII (May, 1964), pp. 235-59.

Eugène Emmanuel Lemercier

Lemercier, Eugène Emmanuel. *Letters of a Soldier: 1914-1915,* with an Introduction by A. Clutton-Brock and a Preface by André Chevrillon. London: Constable, 1917.

_____. *Lettres d'un Soldat (Août 1914-Avril 1915),* Preface de André Chevrillon. Paris: Librairie Chapelot, 1916.

_____. *Notes (1905-1915) Suives de Lettres Inédits, Avec Notice Biographique de M. André Michel.* Paris: Gerger-Levrault, 1924.

————. *A Soldier of France to His Mother: Letters from the Trenches on the Western Front,* translated with an Introduction by Theodore Stanton. Chicago: A. C. McClurg, 1917.

Litz, A. Walton. *Introspective Voyager: The Poetic Development of Wallace Stevens.* New York: Oxford Univ. Press, 1972.

Morse, Samuel French. "Lettres d'un Soldat," *Dartmouth College Library Bulletin, 4 n.s. (December, 1961), pp. 44-50.*

Donald Evans

Cook, Howard Willard. *Our Poets of Today.* New York: Moffatt, Yard and Co., 1918.

Damon, S. Foster. *Amy Lowell: A Chronicle,* Boston: Houghton, Mifflin, 1935.

Evans, Donald. *The Art of Donald Evans,* by "Cornwall Hollis." New York: N.L. Brown, 1916.

————. *Discords.* Philadelphia: Brown Brothers, 1912.

————. *Ironica.* New York: N. L. Brown, 1919.

————. *Nine Poems from Valitudinarium.* Philadelphia: N. L. Brown, 1916.

————. *Sonnets from the Patagonian: The Street of Little Hotels.* New York: Claire Marie, 1914.

————. *Sonnets from the Patagonian* (Revised). New York: N. L. Brown, 1918.

————. *Two Deaths in the Bronx.* Philadelphia: N. L. Brown, 1916.

Fields, Kenneth Wayne. "Past Masters: Walter Conrad Arensberg and Donald Evans," *Southern Review,* VI.2, n.s. (April, 1970), pp. 317-39.

Kay-Scott, Cyril. [Frederick Creighton Wellmann]. *Life is Too Short: An Autobiography.* New York: Lippincott, 1943.

Laforgue, Jules, *Selected Writings of Jules Laforgue,* edited and translated by William J. Smith. New York: Grove Press, 1956.

LeGallienne, Richard. *The Romantic Nineties.* Garden City, N.Y.: Doubleday, Page and Co., 1925.

Ramsay, Warren. *Jules Laforgue and the Ironic Inheritnce.* New York: Oxford Univ. Press, 1953.

Ryskamp, Charles, ed. *Wilde and the Nineties: An Essay and an Exhibition.* Princeton: Princeton Univ. Library, 1966.

Thomson, Vance. *French Portraits: Being Appreciations of the Writers of Young France.* Boston: Badger and Co., 1900.

Wilde, Oscar. *The Complete Works of Oscar Wilde,* with an Introduction by Vyvyan Holland. London: Collins, 1948, 1973.

Winters, Yvor. *Forms of Discovery: Critical and Historical Essays on the Form of the Short Poem in English.* Denver: Alan Swallow, 1967.

Wood, Clement. *Poets of America.* New York: Dutton, 1925.

William Carlos Williams

Breslin, James. *William Carlos Williams: An American Artist.* New York: Oxford Univ. Press, 1970.

Dijkstra, Bram. *The Hieroglyphics of a New Speech: Cubism, Stieglitz, and the Early Poetry of William Carlos Williams.* Princeton: Princeton Univ. Press, 1969.

Friedman, Melvin J. and John B. Vickery, eds. *The Shaken Realist: Essays in Modern Literature in Honor of Frederick J. Hoffman.* Baton Rouge: Louisiana State Univ. Press, 1970.

Gallup, Donald. "T.S.Eliot and Ezra Pound: Collaborators in Letters," *Poetry Australia,* 32 (1970), pp. 53-80.

Guimond, James. *The Art of William Carlos Williams: A Discovery and Possession of America.* Urbana: Univ. of Illinois Press, 1968.

Hardie, Jack. "Hibiscus and the Spaniard of the Rose: Williams' Dialogue wth Wallace Stevens," *William Carlos Williams Newsletter,* Vol. 4, No. 2 (Fall 1978), pp. 20-24.

Kenner, Hugh. *A Homemade World.* New York: Knopf, 1975.

Koch, Vivienne. *William Carlos Williams.* New York: New Directions, 1950.

Mariani, Paul L. *William Carlos Williams: The Poet and His Critics.* Chicago: American Library Association, 1975.

Mitchell, Roger S. "Wallace Stevens' 'Spaniard of the Rose': William Carlos Williams," *Notes and Queries,* n.s. 10 (October, 1961), pp. 381-2.

Simpson, Louis. *Three on the Tower: The Lives and Works of Ezra Pound, T.S. Eliot, and William Carlos Williams.* New York: Morrow, 1975.

Tomlinson, Charles, ed. *William Carlos Williams: A Critical Anthology.* Middlesex, England: Penguin, 1972.

Wallace, Emily Mitchell. *A Bibliography of William Carlos Williams.* Middletown, Conn.: Wesleyan Univ. Press, 1968.

Weaver, Mike. *William Carlos Williams: The American Background.* Cambridge Univ. Press, 1971.

Williams, William Carlos. "America, Whitman, and the Art of Poetry," *Poetry Journal,* VIII.i (November, 1917), pp. 27-36.

_____. *The Autobiography of William Carlos Williams.* New York: New Directions, 1951.

_____. *Collected Early Poems.* New York: New Directions, 1966.

_____. *I Wanted to Write a Poem: The Autobiography of the Works of a Poet,* reported and edited by Edith Heal. New York: New Directions, 1958.

_____. *Imaginations,* edited with an Introduction by Webster Schott. New York: New Directions, 1970.

_____. *In the American Grain.* New York: New Directions, 1925, 1935.

_____. *Selected Essays.* New York: Random House, 1954.

Books by and about Other of Stevens's Acquaintances

Bynner, Witter. *Selected Poems,* edited and with a Critical Introduction by Richard Wilbur; Biographical Introduction by James Kraft. New York: Farrar, Straus, Giroux, 1978.

Ficke, Arthur Davison. *Sonnets of a Portrait-Painter.* New York: Mitchell Kennerly, 1914.

Hartley, Marsden. *Adventures in the Arts: Informal Chapters on Painters, Vaudeville, and Poets.* New York: Boni and Liveright, 1921.

Kaplan, Justin. *Lincoln Steffens: A Biography.* New York: Simon and Schuster, 1974.

Knoll, Robert E. *Robert McAlmon: Expatriate Publisher and Writer,* with a Foreword by William Carlos Williams. Lincoln: University of Nebraska Press, 1959.

Kreymborg, Alfred. *Blood of Things: A Second Book of Free Forms.* New York: N. L. Brown, 1920.

_____. ed. *Lyric America: An Anthology of American Poetry (1630-1930).* New York: Coward-McCann, 1930.

_____. *Mushrooms: A Book of Free Forms.* New York: John Marshall, 1916.

_____. *Our Singing Strength: An Outline of American Poetry (1620-1930).* New York: Coward-McCann, 1930.

_____. *Plays for Poet-Mimes.* New York: The Other Press, 1918.

Liebowitz, Herbert A. *Musical Impressions: Selections from Paul Rosenfeld's Criticism.* New York: Hill and Wang, 1969.

Lindsay, Robert O. *Witter Bynner: A Bibliography.* Albuquerque: University of New Mexico Press, 1967.

Lyon, James K. *Bertolt Brecht's American Cicerone.* Bonn: Bouvier Verlag Herbert Grundmann, 1978.

Macy, John. *The Spirit of American Literature.* New York: Boni and Liveright, 1913.

McAlmon, Robert and Kay Boyle. *Being Geniuses Together, 1920-1930.* New York: Doubleday, 1968.

Rosenfeld, Paul, *By Way of Art: Criticisms of Music, Literature, Painting, Sculpture, and the Dance.* New York: Coward-McCann, 1928.

_____. *Men Seen: Twenty-Four Modern Authors.* New York: Dial Press, 1925.

_____. *Musical Chronicle (1917-1923).* New York: Harcourt, Brace, 1923.

_____. *Port of New York: Essays on Fourteen American Moderns.* New York: Harcourt, Brace, 1924.

Sanborn, Pitt *The Autobiography of Lincoln Steffens.* New York: Harcourt, Brace, 1931.

Zigrosser, Carl. *My Own Shall Come to Me: A Personal Memoir and Picture Chronicle.* Casa Laura, 1971.

Index

Anderson, Hans Christian, 47
Arensberg, Walter Conrad: 19-53 *passim;* 67; connection with Stevens, 20-22; character, 27-28; as poet, 45-48. *See also:* Chess, Cryptography, Dante, Shakespeare/Bacon Controversy
Armory Show, The (1913), 5-7, 19, 21-22

Bacon, Sir Francis. *See* Shakespeare/Bacon Controversy
Barnes, Djuna, 23
Baudelaire, Charles, 70
Beardsley, Aubrey, 15, 24, 74
Beethoven, Ludwig van, 58
Bernhardt, Sarah, 69
Bibelot, 25
Blindman, The, 27, 29, 35, 37-39, 46, 101 n.70
Bombois, Camille, 22
Booth, William Stone, 30
Braque, Georges, 22
Broom, 86, 87
Brown, Milton, 34
Buffet-Picabia, Gabrielle, 26
Buttel, Robert, 16, 71
Bynner, Witter, 66, 68

Chess, 28-30
Claire Marie Press, The, 4, 7, 17, 68
Contact, 86
Covert, John, 15, 26, 30
Cryptography, 30-33
Cubism, 22, 33

Dada, 26, 27, 28, 41, 46
Dante, 21, 31, 48-53
Debussy, Claude, 46
Demuth, Charles, 23
de Zayas, Marius, 23
Dijkstra, Bram, 23
Dodge, Mabel, 5, 7, 23
Dolls: as Nineties icons, 15; as mechanomorphic images, 37
Dolly Sisters, The, 28

Dreier, Katherine, 30
Duchamp, Marcel, 15, 23, 26-41 *passim;* meets Stevens, 35; use of titles, 33-34; readymades, 38-40; "Nude Descending a Staircase," 6, 26, 33-34, 35; "Fountain," 36, 32-41
Duncan, Isadora, 28

Eliot, T.S., 73, 80
Ellmann, Richard, 15, 74
Evans, Donald, 3-17 *passim,* 65-75 *passim;* quoted, 6, 10, 68, 70, 105 (n.9). *See also:* Claire Marie Press, *Sonnets from the Patagonian*

Ferrer School, The, 22, 99 (n.20)
Ficke, Arthur Davison, 68; on Donald Evans, 9, 65, 67; on Louise (Norton) Varèse, 9; on Stevens, 65
Fitch, Albert Parker, (n.4) 104-5 (n.4)
French language, 26, 27
Fussell, Paul, 60, 62
Futurism, 33, 36

Gallup, Donald, 80
Gleizes, Albert, 26, 33
Gray, David, 25

Homer, William Innes, 27

Imagism, 13, 14, 79
Ivins, Jr., William M., 29, 30

Journalism: occupation of the "Patagonians," 4-7; occupation of Stevens' Harvard friends, 21

Kees, Weldon, 21
Kent, Rockwell, 99 (n.20)
Kimball, Fiske, 20
Kreymborg, Alfred, 15, 17, 23-24, 29, 30, 65, 69, 72, 86
Kuh, Katharine, 28

Latimer, Emily, 104 (n.4)
Le Gallienne, Richard, 69, 105 (n.19)
Lemercier, Eugène Emmanuel, 55-64 *passim*
Little Review, The, 85, 86
Litz, A. Walton, 11, 33, 55, 56, 66, 73, 83
Lovelace, Richard, 65
Lowell, Amy, 10, 28, 65, 68, 104 (n.2), 105 (n.15)
Luhan, Mabel Dodge. *See* Dodge, Mabel

Maeterlinck, Maurice, 15
Mallarmé, Stéphane, 49
Marinoff, Fania, 9
Matisse, Henri, 19
McAlmon, Robert, 86
Merritt, Abraham, 6
Modern School, The, 22
Monroe, Harriet, 16, 19, 41, 57, 58, 59, 82, 86
Moore, Marianne, 24
Morse, Samuel French, 49, 50, 56
Mosher, Thomas Bird, 25

Nineties (English 1890s), 8, 10-13, 24-25, 40-41, 45, 71, 72. *See also:* Wilde, Oscar; Whistler, James Abbott McNeill.
Norton, Allen, 5, 11, 23, 29; *Saloon Sonnets* reviewed, 10; *See also: Rogue*
Norton, Charles Eliot, 20-21
Norton, Louise. *See* Varèse, Louise (Norton)

O'Neill, Rose, 104 (n.4)
Others, 27, 45, 70, 77, 82

Pach, Walter, 22, 30, 35, 99 (n.20)
Picabia, Francis, 15, 23, 26, 36
Picasso, Pablo, 19
Plato, 78
Poetry, 19, 83. *See also:* Monroe, Harriet
Pope, Alexander, 74
Pound, Ezra, 12-14 *passim,* 16, 33, 65, 80, 88, 104 (n.2); "Hugh Selwyn Mauberley," 12, 13; on Yeats, 13, 14

Ray, Man, 23, 29, 30, 33
Reyher, Ferdinand, 65, 93, 97 (n.1)
Ridge, Lola, 23
Riddel, Joseph, 34, 62, 89, 103 (n.20)
Robinson, Edwin Arlington, 65, 104 (n.2)
Roché, Henri-Pierre, 26, 29
Roché, Juliette, 26
Rodin, Auguste, 19
Rogue, 5, 7, 11, 17, 21, 23, 24-26, 27, 29, 41, 46, 77
Rongwrong, 27, 29
Rosenfeld, Paul, 65, 69
Russell, Lillian, 28

Sanborn, Pitts, 10, 21, 23, 24, 26, 35, 65, 93, 101 (n.70)

Santayana, George, 13, 21
Schamberg, Morton, 15, 23, 36
Shakespeare/Bacon Controversy, 30, 46
Sheeler, Charles, 23
Society of Independent Artists, 19, 35, 36, 37
Sonnets from the Patagonian: reviews of, 10, 11; quoted, 8, 9, 69, 70, 71, 72, 73. *See also:* Evans, Donald
Southard, Elmer Ernest, 29
Spinoza, 59
Stein, Gertrude, 7-10, 67, 71
Stella, Joseph, 23
Stevens, Holly, 29, 66
Stevens, Wallace. Works by:
  Anecdote of the Jar, 39-41
  Bantams in Pine-Woods, 9, 31
  Bowl, Cat, and Broomstick, 22
  Carlos Among the Candles, 39, 84
  Comedian as the Letter C, The, 9, 55, 66, 73, 93
  Cy Est Pourtraicte, Madame Ste Ursule, et Les Unze Mille Vierges, 11, 25
  Death of a Soldier, The, 56, 59, 60
  Disillusionment of Ten O'Clock, 6, 24, 25, 78, 79
  Dolls, 3, 11, 14-16, 79
  Domination of Black, 34, 46
  Earthy Anecdote, 22, 30
  Emperor of Ice-Cream, The, 31, 66
  Esthétique du Mal, 74, 86
  Fabliau of Florida, 34
  For an Old Woman in a Wig, 49-53
  Headache, 32-33, 79
  Hibiscus on the Sleeping Shores, 86
  "I have lived so long with the rhetoricians," 3
  Idea of Order at Key West, The, 87
  Infernale, 3
  Lettres d'un Soldat, 55-64
  Lunar Paraphrase, 55-64
  Man Whose Pharynx Was Bad, The, 34, 73
  Meditation, 70
  Metaphors of a Magnifico, 61
  Moment of Light, 98 (n.20)
  Le Monocle de Mon Oncle, 9, 16, 31, 34, 37, 50, 66, 70-75
  Noble Rider and the Sound of Words, The, 61, 78
  Notes Toward a Supreme Fiction, 53, 62-64
  Nuances of a Theme by Williams, 85
  Oak Leaves are Hands, 66
  Paltry Nude Starts on a Spring Voyage, The, 34
  Planet on the Table, The, 66
  Primordia, 39, 58, 84
  Romance for a Demoiselle Lying in the Grass, 36
  Six Significant Landscapes, 82, 83
  Snow Man, The, 58

Sonatina to Hans Christian, 47-48
Stars at Tallapoosa, 87-89
Sunday Morning, 3, 16, 17, 50, 73
Tea, 25
Tea at the Palaz of Hoon, 34, 58
Three Travelers Watch a Sunrise, 82, 84
Weeping Burgher, The, 68, 73
Worms at Heaven's Gate, The, 77-81
Stieglitz, Alfred, 19, 23, 28, 36
Sunwise Turn Bookshop, The, 23

Tashjian, Dickran, 23, 40
Theis, Otto, 68, 105 (n.14)
391, 29, 46
Tice, Clara, 26
Titles, their use by Stevens and Duchamp, 33-35
TNT, 46
Trend, 4, 11, 17, 21, 23, 24, 27, 41, 67
291, 36

Varèse, Edgar, 26
Varèse, Louise (Norton), 3, 4, 9, 10, 23-24, 38, 67, 68
Van Vechten, Carl, 3-17 *passim;* 24, 26; on

Armory Show, 6; on Donald Evans, 5, 9, 67; meets Stevens, 95 (n.5)
Vendler, Helen, 73, 104 (n.22)
Verlaine, Paul, 8, 59

War: effect on Stevens' acquaintances, 26, 29, 70-71; in Stevens' poetry, 55-64
Whistler, James Abbott McNeill, 25
Wilde, Oscar, 69, 70, 72-73, 74, 105 (n.19), 106 (nn.21, 33)
Williams, William Carlos, 12, 23, 26, 39-41, 52, 53, 66, 77-91
  Works by:
  Eyeglasses, The, 87-89
  El Hombre, 84-85
  Postlude, 79
  Red Wheelbarrow, The, 39-40
  Rose, The, 89
  Summer Song, 83
  This Florida: 1924, 86
  Wanderer, The, 82
Winters, Yvor, 66

Yeats, William Butler, 11-16, 74

Zigrosser, Carl, 99 (n.20)